The Practice of
Watercolour Painting

J. M. W. Turner *The Devil's Bridge, Pass of
St Gothard* 1802. Watercolour, pencil and
body colour 18½ × 12½ in./471 × 318 mm.
British Museum, London.

Leslie Worth

The Practice of Watercolour Painting

Pitman, London
Watson—Guptill Publications, New York

PITMAN PUBLISHING LIMITED
39 Parker Street, London WC2B 5PB

Associated Companies
Copp Clark Ltd, Toronto · Pitman Publishing Co. SA (Pty) Ltd, Johannesburg
Pitman Publishing New Zealand Ltd, Wellington · Pitman Publishing Pty
Ltd, Melbourne · Sir Isaac Pitman Ltd, Nairobi

© Leslie Worth 1977

First published in Great Britain 1977

Published simultaneously in the United States by Watson-Guptill
Publications, a division of Billboard Publications Inc., One Astor Plaza,
New York, N.Y. 10036

Worth, Leslie
    The practice of watercolour painting.
    1. Water-color painting—Technique
    I. Title
    751.4'22   ND2420

    UK ISBN 0–273–00115–9

    US ISBN 8230–4383–5

Text set in 12/13 pt Monotype Bembo, printed by photolithography,
and bound in Great Britain at The Pitman Press, Bath

Contents

Acknowledgements

The idea for this book grew from a series of six articles which I wrote for the *Artist* magazine in the summer of 1974, and I am indebted to the Editor, Mr Peter Garrard, for suggesting this and allowing me to use the articles.

I gratefully acknowledge the cooperation of the Trustees of the British Museum, the Tate Gallery, the Victoria and Albert Museum and the custodians of the Daitoku-ji collection, Kyoto, for kindly allowing me to reproduce paintings in their possession.

I am also indebted to Winsor & Newton for providing information and allowing me to reproduce plates of their materials. To Wiggins Teape and the Inveresk Paper Company for assistance on paper manufacture, to Thames and Hudson and to artists and collectors for their kind cooperation. To Mrs Jo Smith who typed the manuscript, to my wife who read it and advised me. To Mr Robert Cross who took the photographs. To Mrs Jo Christian and Mr David Lewis, the Arts and Crafts Editor of Pitman Publishing, and his staff for their kind assistance, and to all those other people without whose help and encouragement this book would never have been completed.

1 Introduction

> I am here on behalf of my own profession, and I trust it
> is with no intrusive spirit that I now stand before you; but
> I am anxious that the world should be inclined to look to
> painters for information on painting . . .
>
> > John Constable,
> > First Lecture at the
> > Royal Institution,
> > 26 May 1836

It was when I was a small child that I first began painting with watercolours. I cannot remember exactly when; but there must have been a moment when, like other children, I discovered for the first time the fascination of the wash of colour, appearing as if by magic on the paper under the impact of the cheap squirrel-hair brush. I do recall later, as a schoolboy, painting pictures from imagination; my first steps were gauche and tentative and there was nothing in those arid stains of colour that I would be proud to recall now.

It was when I was about twelve that I discovered 'real' water-colours. There was an artist named Britton whose paintings hung in the art gallery in Plymouth. They were lush, romantic paintings of Dartmoor, purple heather, encrusted forms of granite rocks and shimmering moorland streams. I stared enviously at those paintings, wishing I could paint like that.

Later, as an art student, I came across the English watercolour school for the first time, in a book. I never dreamed that such beautiful things had existed. The reproductions were second rate, but I did not know that, all I knew was that the curtain had been lifted an inch or two and beyond lay a territory whose existence I had never suspected, and the boundaries of which I could not define, but which beckoned irresistibly. Painting has brought many exciting discoveries, but nothing has moved me quite so much as watercolours, although in spite of the early infatuation my art education lay in other directions.

My training as an art student was long and academic, first in Devonshire and later at the Royal College of Art where I painted nudes and still lifes in oil. During that time no one ever taught me how to paint in watercolour. I was my own master and pupil, and when, in my late twenties, I began to use it again, it was like returning to my first love. It was the beginning of an affair which has lasted ever since.

This book is an attempt to describe something of that experience and to offer some guidelines to the serious student of this absorbing and exasperating medium.

But first of all let me try to put the subject in perspective with a brief account of the role of watercolour painting—or watercolour drawing as it was traditionally called, and which perhaps provides a more accurate description. In many ways watercolour with its essential spontaneity is closer to drawing than it is to oil painting, where the forms are built up over a longer period and if unsatisfactory may be erased and built up again.

Painting or drawing in pigments ground in water and bound with some natural substance, e.g. gum, starch or honey, was

Plate 1 *Nebamon hunting accompanied by his Daughter* 1500 B.C. Watercolour on plaster (fresco) 32 × 38 in./813 × 965 mm. British Museum, London.
A fragment of wall painting from the tomb of Nebamon, King of Egypt. The painter would have used pigments ground in water, bound with a size or distemper medium.

probably the earliest colour method used by man in an attempt to record his existence.

The earliest known paintings, the pre-historic cave art of Altamira and Lascaux, were probably painted with simple organic materials: reds and ochres from the soil and black from the carbonized bone or wood from their fires, ground with water and, we suspect, applied with 'mops' made from moss or fur from the skins of animals.

The painters of ancient Egypt as far back in time as 4,500 B.C. worked in watercolours in the wall paintings of the tombs of the Pharaohs. Later, Chinese artists, working within a tradition that was to span thousands of years, developed a highly sophisticated but essentially simple technique of painting with watercolour and ink (*sumi*) on paper and silk. This method probably reached its peak in the work of the Ch'an school of the Sung dynasty during the thirteenth century. Also from the East we have the exquisite miniature paintings of the Persian and Indian schools. These were carried out in body colour, using colours bound in gum, the modelling of the forms produced by minute hatching.

Plate 3 *Lovers on a Terrace* 1750–60. Water-colour on paper 9⅛ × 7 in./232 × 178 mm. Victoria and Albert Museum, London. An Indian painting of the Bilaspur school. Indian painting probably reached its peak during the second half of the eighteenth century. Conceived as a private art, not for public consumption, it was often associated with poetry and sometimes with music. They were painted on paper with water-colours bound in gum. The designs were lightly and exquisitely drawn in and colours built up section by section, the detail hatched in with finely pointed brushes. The coloured border is considered an integral part of the design; often painted in complementary colours, it serves to bind the painting together.

In European painting, the development of the use of water-colours can be traced through medieval manuscripts and Renaissance miniatures, the work of distinguished artists such as Dürer and Rubens, and the emergence of the English topographical school of watercolour drawing in the eighteenth century, to the painting of today. We clearly have a record of a medium that is distinguished as much by its richness as by its diversity and I do not suppose that its possibilities are exhausted.

Naturally, like all the arts, watercolour has had its periods of ascent and of decline. It has been embraced by national consciousness and identified with particular periods of human endeavour, and sometimes too respectfully circumscribed by past records of achievement.

Societies devoted to its advancement have been founded and royal patronage conferred on its practice. It has been overlaid by sophistry and technical accomplishment, as in the nineteenth century when painters attempted to challenge the ascendency of oil painting with watercolours of increased scale and elaboration. While they may have gained in impact, they lost altogether those particular qualities of watercolour which I propose to discuss later.

Watercolour has always played an important role in English

art (although the peak of its excellence covered a span of barely sixty years) and there has been reserved for English artists, along with the Chinese and Japanese, the privilege of understanding its secrets and preserving its practice in a changing world which was no longer interested in its potential.

Despite the long history of painting with water-based colours, it was not until the fifteenth century that watercolour was used as a solo medium in Europe. Even then it continued to be used chiefly for sketches on which the more important oil painting would later be based. It was the English school of landscape painting that most thoroughly exploited the resources of water-colour, and when it was taken up by artists of the stature of Turner it became evident that the medium was capable of surpassing power and lyrical beauty.

It would not be possible in a book of these dimensions to do justice to all the ways in which painting in watercolour has manifested itself, even if I were capable of doing so. Rather, I am more concerned to discuss the medium and its practice in what has become known as the 'English' method (transparent watercolour) and to show how the essential simplicity of this method may be

Plate 4 Nicholas Hilliard *Youth leaning against a Tree* 1588. Watercolour on vellum 5⅜ × 2¾ in./136 × 69 mm. Victoria and Albert Museum, London.
This miniature is painted on vellum. The foundation was a light drawing, over which the colours, thin but full in execution, were laid, shadows hardly being used at all. The full strength of the colour was built up gradually. Miniature painting was an exacting craft and Hilliard left a record of the advice he would give to those who contemplate 'the Arte of Limning':
. . . the best waye and meanes to practice and ataine to skill in limning; in a word befor I exhorteth such to temperance, I meane sleepe not much, watch not much, eat not much, sit not long, use not violent exercise in sports, nor earnest for your recreation, but dancing or bowling, or little of either . . .

INTRODUCTION

Plate 5 John Sell Cotman *The Devil's Bridge, Cardiganshire* 1801. Watercolour 10 × 7 in./254 × 178 mm. Victoria and Albert Museum, London.

Painted when Cotman was a young man of nineteen, from a drawing made on a sketching tour in Wales, this watercolour shows his precocious development and originality of style. His delicate but brilliant counterchange of light and dark was quite unique and thwarted his bid for success throughout his life.

The drawing is built up of transparent washes of colour overlapping one another, then lifted out in parts and strengthened in others until a balance is achieved and the forms begin to crystallize. Final passages are hatched in with fine brushmarks or lifted out with a rag and sharp knife. Later he experimented with a paste medium in order to introduce a tougher, textural quality into the pictures.

capable of extension. After all, this is the basis of all the related techniques and once the essential characteristics have been grasped it can be adapted as the painter thinks fit.

Why is it that after all these centuries of use watercolour still retains a hold on our imaginations and affections? We might be forgiven for assuming that it would have been eclipsed by the technical advances that have distinguished this century and the development of resources at the disposal of the modern painter, but on the contrary, in spite of periods when its position was in doubt, painting in watercolour has persisted and indeed today there is a resurgence of its popularity as a medium.

At this juncture it may be useful to take a look at the basic nature of the medium, overlaid as it has been with elaboration and trickery, and to ask just what it is that is unique about it.

If watercolour is compared with oil or acrylic painting, then the difference in character is immediately apparent. It has always

Plate 6 John Piper *Somerset Place, Bath* 1942. Watercolour, chalk, ink, gouache 18 × 29 in./457 × 737 mm. Tate Gallery, London.

Painted in 1942 when Piper was an official War Artist, this work illustrates his horror at the devastation of war, exemplified in the destruction of this famous Georgian crescent. It is not, however, portrayed in the apocalyptic way that might have been fitting for Rotterdam or Dresden. For all its drama it has a reserve of statement which makes it all the more poignant.

The painting was built up from broad washes of colour, over which a fine pencil drawing was laid (the lines of the window openings are visible). Over this the drawing was given emphasis with Indian ink and a supporting build-up of colour in the threatening sky passages. Further details were picked out by heightening with Chinese white. It is interesting to note the way that in tackling this subject the artist, consciously or unconsciously, evokes the spirit of English topographical drawing but gives it a sense of drama—compare Turner's *Llandaff Cathedral* (Plate 9).

suffered from being regarded by some people (including those who should know better) as the poor relation, which is a rather myopic view. True, it is not identified with great scale or the 'grand manner' in art; it lacks the tactile qualities of oil painting and it has not the same carrying power or sheer presence, but this is not to deny the validity of its own special character. After all, it is as if one condemned the piano for lacking the range of the organ, or, because of its brevity, considered the poem as being in some way inferior to the novel.

I am not trying to put up some elaborate defence for watercolour—I don't have to. I am fully aware of its limitations, after all, I spent long years of apprenticeship painting in oil. The fact that I choose to paint with watercolour is because it is so exactly right for what I wish to say. (Of course I do occasionally paint with oil, if only because I get fed up with wet sleeves!)

I find the medium fascinating because, however much one may claim to be in control, there is always an element of unpredictability. Monet once said that to him painting was like throwing oneself into the water to see if one could swim. I think this is particularly true of watercolour painting; it constitutes a challenge which is always present but which is constantly assuming different guises according to the nature of the subject and conditions, because although all media are to some extent affected by the environmental conditions, heat, humidity, etc., watercolour is more affected than any other. The painter quickly learns that he must match his versatility and resourcefulness to the prevailing conditions, particularly if he is choosing to work out of doors.

7

Plate 7 Paul Nash *Eclipse of the Sunflower*
1945. Watercolour and pencil 16½ × 22½ in./
418 × 571 mm. Victoria and Albert
Museum, London.
Nash had a great interest in the forces that
govern natural life, the rotation of seasons
and how man expresses these in his symbols,
in art and religion. The year before he died,
in failing health, he turned again to these
themes, and this watercolour with its
symbols of life and death is a good example
of this late work. The sunflower head
becomes a rotating sun symbol; the dead
seed-head lies below.

Paul Nash favoured a heavy paper on
which he painted directly with vigorous
strokes, sometimes wetting the paper in
advance, but more frequently hatching
swiftly into the dry surface with crisp
brush strokes.

It is a medium requiring quick decisions in the sense that the
forms must be given their appropriate expression at once. Some
adjustment may be permissible but essentially watercolour
requires careful deliberation, an imaginative projection of what
the painting will look like, and rapid, sure execution.

I find that I can only work in comparatively short spells of an
hour or two because the concentration required is so intense. If I
paint in oil, I can stop halfway through and have a cup of coffee
and go back to it again. Not so with watercolour. I have to go on
without interruption until either the work is complete, or a certain
stage is reached which requires a halt before embarking on the
next.

One quality which watercolour possesses more than any other
medium is the ability to convey a sense of suspended animation:
it can imprison those moments when things are in transition, the
sun appearing behind a bank of cloud, a figure stepping out of
shadow, a bird darting out of a thicket; by bringing these
elements into focus it seals them for all time and by setting them
in equipoise with one another defines the constant within the
transient.

Furthermore, it possesses the quality of mobility. Unlike the
opaque methods of painting where the forms are built up in
separate touches, watercolour allows colour to be drifted across

THE PRACTICE OF WATERCOLOUR PAINTING

the surface with changing momentum and density. Just as a skilful skater will 'feel' the surface of the ice, sometimes speeding across in great skimming movements, sometimes hugging the surface, or contrasting short weaving movements with long glides, so in a similar way the skilled painter reacts to and is aware of the surface of the paper, which is never an anonymous, inert plane. This change of momentum is, as it were, 'frozen' on to the paper and, calligraphic in essence, it bears the mark of impulse in perpetuity.

At the heart of all this lies the essential simplicity of water-colour, its ability to convey information or mood or emotion directly, without fuss or the interpolation of any complex means or medium, so that its message is quite unambiguous.

Its economy of expression to me is beautiful. If I could be proud of having possessed one quality in the practice of water-colour I should choose this. Matisse once said that he would like to paint as a bird sings—simply, naturally, unaffectedly. These are the qualities that the best watercolours possess; these are the qualities we should try to preserve in our practice.

It is by nature a small-size medium but can suggest great size. Turner's *S. Giorgio Maggiore from the Dogana* measures only eight inches by eleven, but its scale is limitless.

It can be capable of surprising power, delicate but not insipid. It calls for a sensibility alive to its complementary qualities, where sharp crisp touches contrast with soft diaphanous surfaces and tran-quil areas are foiled by areas of activity. If one watches a good

Plate 8 Susan Hawker *Meadows, Steeple Aston* 1975. Watercolour and pencil 6 × 10 in./ 152 × 254 mm. Author's collection. A skilful, economical drawing in warm and cool greys, built up with a light pencil drawing as a foundation. The colours do not so much describe as bind together the forms and sometimes emphasize and at other times obscure the shapes of the trees and cottages which are the subject matter of the drawing. It is painted on a cartridge paper, much of which is left untouched. This technique is reminiscent of some of Cézanne's drawings where the virgin paper serves as a key to the painted areas.

THE PRACTICE OF WATERCOLOUR PAINTING

Plate 9 J. M. W. Turner *Llandaff Cathedral, South Wales* 1795–6. Pencil and watercolour 14 × 10⅛ in./356 × 257 mm. British Museum, London.

In June and July of 1795, when Turner was twenty, he went on a sketching tour of South Wales and this painting is based on a sketchbook drawing done on the spot. It demonstrates Turner's understanding of the tradition of topographical drawing in the early nineteenth century. The design shows strong counterbalanced areas of light and dark, warm and cool. A light pencil drawing, fairly complete, was first made on the paper and a wash of warm colour applied overall to give a key to the drawing and establish in some measure the warm sienna areas of masonry and cloud. Further washes of cool and warm colour were applied, linking sky and architecture. This was continued, building up in strength and with no attempt made to separate out the forms. Gradually the forms were defined in reference to the overall scheme. At times areas of colour were washed out or lifted, as in the front of the building. Finally, the details of architecture and figures were defined with a fine brush and parts picked out with judicious use of body colour. Occasionally a pen with thinned down ink was used to define some of the architectural details. All this was done, of course, some months later in his studio in London.

Plate 10 *A Shower of Leaves* 1973. Watercolour 14½ × 21 in./368 × 533 mm. Private collection.

This landscape was painted on the spot one Sunday morning in November at Headley in Surrey. It is largish, almost Half Imperial or A2 size, painted on 90 lb (185 gsm) Saunders Not surface mould-made paper which was rather spongy in texture. The colours are soft, warm olive greens and umbers and blue/violet greys.

The landscape lay under a lowering sky which threatened rain at any time. A warm westerly wind blew fitfully and I painted shielded by a large beech tree to the left.

I worked initially without much enthusiasm, wondering what to do with this featureless landscape, and I had practically decided to call it a day and go home. Suddenly a tremendous burst of wind with spots of rain sprang up. Instantly the air all round me was full of whirling leaves. Here was my subject. I worked quickly—it was all over in five minutes.

The fine lines of rain across the distant trees were scored with a sharp knife. The rain has left bleached out light spots in the sky.

Plate 11 J. M. W. Turner *Venice: S. Giorgio Maggiore from the Dogana* 1819. Watercolour 8 × 11 in./203 × 279 mm. British Museum, London.
Painted in Venice in 1819 during the period from August to the following January. This was Turner's first visit to Venice. Most of his work was done in sketchbooks, in pencil, building up information for future work, although this drawing bears the evidence of having been done on the spot. It is a miracle of restrained and direct drawing. The colour and position of the sun suggest early morning and a mist is lying over the lagoon. A pale wash of oyster colour was laid over the paper, linking sky and water together. When this was dry the distant shape of the buildings was drawn in, working towards the church on the right, the ripple of sunlight on the water in the foreground was lifted out with a damp rag, and the reflection of the campanile added. Finally, with sharp, liquid touches of colour, the boats were drawn in.

watercolourist at work, the play of brushwork is infinitely various, the pace of character and expression frequently changing although the brush may scarcely be lifted from the paper.

But above all the delight of watercolour lies in its restraint and its prime attribute is lucidity. It requires a mind that is keen and reflective and can envisage the final result—but not too well, for one must be aware of what is happening beneath the brush and be prepared to take advantage of the unpremeditated development. This lovely and delicate medium has a will of its own, it can be wooed but not bludgeoned into doing what we would have it do.

Its beauty lies in the way in which its limitations are realized and explored. It is a matter of swift decisions, the calculation of opposites of light and dark masses and linear patterns, governed by the underlying paper, the fluency of the water, and the density and penetration of the stain.

H. J. Paris, *English Watercolour Painters.*

2 Materials

THE PHYSICAL PROPERTIES OF THE MEDIUM

> . . . a first hand knowledge of sound technique is of enormous assistance to the painter in enabling him to express his intentions with accuracy; and the knowledge that he has utilized the best possible means to attain his ends and to ensure permanence brings an increase of confidence.
>
> Ralph Mayer, *The Artist's Handbook of Materials and Techniques.*

Light behaviour

Painting in any medium is subject to the physical laws governing light behaviour, and watercolour, because of its transparency and relatively uncomplex process, is particularly susceptible to these laws. It is important that the student should be aware of this at the outset.

We know, of course, that daylight or white light is composed of a number of varying wavelengths, which in themselves produce different sensations or reactions on the retina, thereby giving rise to different colour sensations, from yellow to violet, called 'the spectrum'.

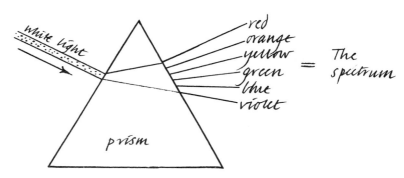

Fig 1 White light passing through a prism.

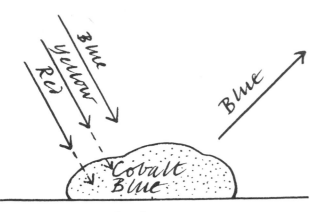

Fig 2 Light refraction.

Consider the three primary colours, red, yellow, blue. Colours which fall into any of these categories appear so because they reflect the colours of one group, while absorbing the colours of the other two.

For example, if light falls on cobalt blue, most of the blue rays are reflected and the remainder (the yellow/red end of the spectrum) are absorbed. This is true of all colours, the specific behaviour varying somewhat from colour to colour.

If more colours are involved then the interaction of absorption and reflection is more complex, and is continued beyond the point where the painter can control it. You may have noticed in some paintings employing a pointillist technique that at a distance there is a greying or chalky effect. The colours are beginning to cancel themselves out as through the optical mixing they reflect more and more white light along with the main colours. Obversely, when colours are physically mixed then the degree of light absorption is increased, and in direct ratio to the number of colours involved. This is known as the subtractive law, because increased mixing subtracts still more colour waves. Consequently luminosity or brilliance of colour is diminished the more one mixes colour. After all, one cannot add colour to an already light colour and make it lighter!

If, however, one uses a transparent medium, say coloured light or white light passing through a prism, then rays of light are not absorbed but are added (or rather, strictly speaking, divided into constituent parts). This is known as the additive law.

It follows from this that the purest transmission of colour is through the medium of light, as in the effulgence of a sunset. The next purest form of colour is to be found in the suspension of colour particles in a clear liquid (an example of this occurs if a glass of wine is held up to the light). Therefore, the maximum colour transmission will be obtained through a medium which has no colouring matter itself and allows the maximum dispersal of colour particles. Here we are at the crux of the matter, for this is the essential characteristic of watercolour.

We take refined colour pigment, grind it exceedingly fine, suspend it in an aqueous solution such as gum, then with one of the purest elements, clear water, float it across a white surface. The water evaporates, leaving minute particles of colour embedded in the paper, but of so fine a consistency that the rays of light striking the paper are reflected with little loss of brilliance.

We have therefore embodied in our medium the three basic elements—earth (pigment), water (the vehicle), and, allowing for the transmission of colour, air. It is from the physical and metaphysical co-mingling of these elements that the art of watercolour is born. Let us examine these elements more closely for a moment, before we pass on to consider the painting material in detail.

The support
The most important factor to consider is the support, the ground for the painting, which in our case is usually paper.

If a wash of colour is spread on a hard smooth ground, such as a gesso panel or white card, the colour is identifiable but inert and lacking in vitality. The surface is uniform and the angle of reflection of light is equal to the angle of incidence. On the other hand, on a good white handmade paper the same wash of colour appears more lively. This is partly because the variations in the surface allow minute areas of white paper to reflect white light along with the prevailing colour, enhancing the luminosity of the colour. Another result of the irregularity of the surface is that rays of coloured light are reflected irregularly, setting up minute oscillations of colour which mutually excite one another, creating a vibrant surface of colour.

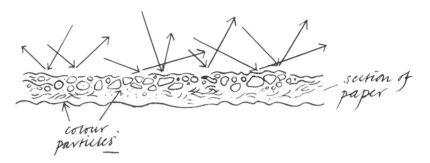

Fig 3 Light reflected at various angles.

The student must experiment with different surfaces to discover the most satisfactory balance between luminosity of colour and suitability of texture. This will be discussed further in the chapter devoted to paper.

The colour film

To repeat: the underlying principle of watercolour is the reflection of light from a white surface through a film of colour. The strength of the colour statement depends on:

1. The initial amount of colour saturation
2. The degree of thinning out
3. The amount of white surface penetration

Strength of colour may be achieved either by brushing on a strong colour value, or by brushing on repeated layers of colour,

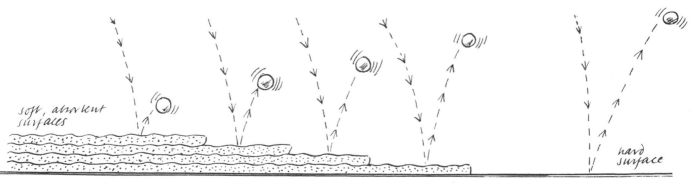

Fig 4 Light reflection.

building up the density. Of course, using the latter method, as the density of the colour is increased so the luminosity decreases.

An analogy may be helpful here. If a rubber ball is dropped on to a hard inert surface the ball will rebound almost to the same height, but a blanket spread on this hard surface would diminish the rebound, and as further layers of blanket were added the rebound would be proportionately reduced until there was none at all.

Substitute paper for the hard surface, a film of colour for the blanket and rays of light for the ball, and I hope the lesson will be clear. Obviously the problem is to achieve some balance between the maximum degree of colour saturation and the minimum application of layers of colour.

The vehicle

This term is generally defined as the liquid carrier of pigments in paint. Strictly speaking it means the liquids used as ingredients in the manufacture, which in our case are gum arabic to provide adhesion for the paint particles and probably glycerine, which keeps the pigments moist and soluble, but here we are chiefly concerned with the means of dispersal, which is relatively uncomplicated in essence, being simply pure water.

There is not a great deal that can be said about the choice of this particular element, except that it should be clean, free from impurities and changed frequently during use. As a general rule, if you would not drink it, don't paint with it!

Some writers on watercolour practice suggest that students should use only distilled water, this being the purest available, and most advise the avoidance of sea water or other sorts of water whose purity may be suspect in one way or another. I am not convinced that distilled water is essential, I cannot claim to be that fastidious, but I would not recommend sea water. I did once arrive on a beach in Dorset ready to paint, and with paper invitingly stretched found that I had left my materials at home, so, with a child's upturned bucket as a palette and with three colours and a cheap brush bought from a gift shop, I painted with sea water! However, although as far as I am aware this watercolour has never shown any obvious signs of dissolution, I would never advise students to follow this example.

Fig 5 Minimal materials.

When I am working in the studio I like to have a plastic bowl with clean water in it as well as a jar. I can then rinse the brushes in the bowl and use the water in the jar as the medium. This requires less frequent changing of water and keeps the colour cleaner.

If you are beginning to paint with watercolours you will discover that the control of water content is the most exacting part of the craft. It is the fluidity of the colour which gives the medium its characteristic beauty. Without this quality watercolours are reduced to mere lifeless stains on the paper, but to strike a cautionary note, don't overdo it.

The water content determines the degree of colour strength (saturation), the transparency or opacity of the colour, the quality of emphasis of a passage, the spatial significance and finally, the movement of colour across the paper, the flow, drift, spread or however one chooses to describe this particular characteristic.

I would advise students to try some simple experiments designed to improve control of the water content.

Using only one or two colours, preferably of a strong, determinable nature, such as indigo or sepia, take a largish brush, no. 8 or 10, and with a well stretched sheet of paper on your board, charge your brush with colour and brush the paint out in broad areas, changing direction as you apply it.

At first, the proportion of pigment to water will be high, giving you a strong, dense stain. Continue, but gradually increasing the water content, brushing up against the previously painted areas, until some areas of paper are faint washes of transparent colour. Carry on with exercises like this for several days, varying the colours used and their density. Consciously aim to work initially with as strong a saturation of colour as possible and gradually diminish in strength. Do not concern yourself with representing anything and endeavour to achieve a combination of the maximum exuberance of surface consistent with the greatest measure of control. If you get into a mess, don't worry, put it to one side and try again. At the end of the week spread your pieces of paper out on the floor, or pin them on to the wall, and try to extract some general principles of procedure from your efforts.

You can vary the exercises by combining washed areas with broad hatchings of colour, superimposed on one another in order to discover how one may employ contrasting areas of activity on the same surface, and you may experiment by painting into previously dampened areas of paper, watching how the colour spreads and disperses on the paper. Tilt the board to observe its behaviour.

Remember that if you add colour to a previously wet surface (which is one of the most difficult and hazardous ploys in water-colour painting) the water content of the added colour should be less than that of the area which is to receive it.

Paper
This is the support commonly used for painting watercolours. We have seen earlier that other materials may also be used but here we are concerned with paper and the various types that are most suitable for our purposes.

Nowadays the manufacture of paper employs a vast and complex industry serving all needs, but for much of its history paper was handmade and it is with the small percentage of handmade or mould-made paper that we are chiefly concerned.

The industry defines paper as 'A sheet or continuous web of material formed by the deposition of vegetable, mineral, animal or synthetic fibres or their mixtures with or without the addition of other substances . . .'. (Robert Higham, *A Handbook of Paper-making*.) If we were to examine it under a microscope it would reveal itself as a web-like mass of interlaced fibres. When we paint it is these minute interstices which retain the particles of colour brushed over the surface.

The best paper for watercolour work is made from pure linen rag, although nowadays cotton is used to a large extent. This is boiled and beaten to separate the fibres until it is a pulp, which is picked up on a fine copper mesh screen.

Plate 12 Demonstration painting. This was devised as an exercise to demonstrate a range of technical possibilities. Paper: T. H. Saunders handmade Rough, 140 lb (295 gsm), 7⅞ × 12¾ in. (200 × 314 mm). Colours: Winsor orange, brown madder, indigo, Winsor blue, sepia.

The paper was first wet all over, and beginning at top centre a pale wash of Winsor orange (this actually produces a strong yellow stain) was brushed on, merging to blue-grey with the addition of Winsor blue, and moving down and across the paper the colour was modulated by additions of madder and indigo and some sepia. This completed the first stage. The paper was allowed to dry, then further washes of colour, starting from the lightest in tone and moving towards the darkest, were added. Sometimes, as in b. on the key, the edge was left crisp, but allowed to merge into a wet area. A good deal of experimenting was carried out, including sponging out of some areas on the right.

Key: The exercise divides approximately left/dark, right/light, top/light, bottom/dark. Numbers 1–7 diagonally indicate increasing depth of tone, light to dark. Actually there are about nine or ten divisions of tone.
a. Lightest area, made by scraping out with a sharp knife.
b. Crisp but delicate edge painted on dry area, but merged with wet ground further down.
c. Blue colour brushed into wet ground and allowed to disperse.
d. Similar but heavier concentrate of colour (sepia), dropped into wet area and 'exploding' more in effect.
e. Pale silhouette of house, set back by virtue of quiet tone value.
f. Tree form drawn in crisply on dry ground, lifting out in tone further down.
g. Maximum build-up of tones (indigo), heavy concentration brushed into damp surface.
Light scratch lines at the foot of the drawing drawn with the tip of a knife.

The manufacture of handmade paper is traditionally carried out by a vatman (nothing to do with taxation) who stands by a large vat measuring about six feet by four by three, in which the heated pulp is kept constantly stirred by a beater.

The sheets of paper are made now by the use of a mould and deckle. The mould is a wooden frame with a copper mesh, of the overall size of the paper, and the deckle is an open frame which fits over the mould, holding the pulp in place. Both are dipped into the vat and, with a practised scooping movement, a small quantity of pulp is picked up. The mould is lifted out and the water allowed to drain away. A gentle sifting action settles the pulp evenly and assists the fibres to interlock. The deckle is then removed and the mould set aside to drain.

Plate 13 A 19th century engraving showing the manufacture of handmade paper. The vatman is shaking the mould to settle the pulp. His assistant, the coucher, is laying felt between sheets of paper. Notice in the foreground the racks and rollers on which the stack of paper is dragged away. The method of producing handmade paper has remained virtually unchanged to the present day.

Next an assistant, known as a coucher, inverts the pulp face downwards on a felt pad and removes the mould. Successive layers of pulp and felt pads are stacked up to a moderate height and then put under a press to remove the excess water. Following this the paper is usually given a sizing of gelatine to complete the process.

Mould-made papers are machine-made, several sheets at a time. A cylinder mould passes through a long vat of paper, picking up the pulp and transferring it to a continuous web or felt. It then passes through heated driers and is reeled at the end of the machine. It will be obvious from this brief description that this process, while quite satisfactory in most respects, will produce a paper of a uniform texture and consistency, unlike the more irregular but sympathetic surface of the handmade papers.

Although mould-made papers are produced by a machine process, the term 'machine-made' always refers to the mass-manufactured papers which are made on the roll and cut to size afterwards.

Paper is usually prepared in one or more of three finishes:

Hot-pressed (HP)	smooth
Not (Not Hot-pressed; in the US known as Cold-pressed, CP)	medium
Rough	coarse

Not and Rough are the two most favoured surfaces for water-colour painting. The Hot-pressed surface is smooth and absorbent and not so suitable for the transparent technique. The grading of the paper is done by the weight of the ream (commonly 500 sheets). This varies from 40–44 lb (110–135 gsm) for a lightweight paper to 400 lb (850 gsm) for the heaviest paper. Intermediate weights run as follows: 72 lb (150 gsm), 90 lb (185 gsm), 133 lb (170 gsm), 140 lb (295 gsm), 200 lb (425 gsm), 240 lb (535 gsm), and 300 lb (635 gsm). These are obtainable in the three surfaces.

Handmade paper is expensive because one is paying for the time of a skilled craftsman engaged in producing it one sheet at a time, and using carefully selected materials. Mould-made paper, produced by a machine, is cheaper, as one might expect, and most students would find this perfectly satisfactory for their purposes.

Plate 14 R. Vivian Pitchforth, R.A., *Rough Sea, Lighthouse Theme* 1968. Watercolour 17 × 23 in./432 × 584 mm. Private collection.
This painting is typical of the artist's inimitable style, the depiction of the stormy sea off the coast is so completely realized and presented in such a simple way that one scarcely notices the acute observation and the strong design holding it together.

Painted directly on an Ingres paper from notes made on the spot. Pitchforth used to paint directly from nature, but more recently works from notes and drawings. He favours pans and tube colours.

Paper mills sell off seconds, papers which have slight blemishes in them. These are called 'retrees' and are cheaper. It is worth contacting a mill to see what they offer in this way.

For the better quality handmade and mould-made paper, traditional sizes are retained in Britain and the US. For other papers, cartridge, etc., the international A sizes are used. A table of sizes follows. These are the mean sizes, actual dimensions of the sheet may be larger.

Antiquarian	31×53 in. $(787 \times 1346$ mm$)$
Double Elephant	27×40 in. $(686 \times 1016$ mm$)$
Elephant	23×28 in. $(584 \times 711$ mm$)$
Imperial	30×22 in. $(762 \times 559$ mm$)$—A1
Half Imperial	15×22 in. $(381 \times 559$ mm$)$—A2
Royal	$19\frac{1}{2} \times 24$ in. $(490 \times 610$ mm$)$

Lightweight drawing papers, generally known as Ingres papers, are produced mainly on the Continent and come in sizes $18\frac{1}{2} \times 25\frac{1}{4}$ in. $(641 \times 470$ mm$)$. Their weight is about 33 lb (104 gsm) and they are made in attractive tints from white to black. They stretch a good deal when wet and can present problems to the uninitiated because of this, but some artists prefer them. I believe R. V. Pitchforth uses an Ingres paper, which is ideally suited to his *premier coup* mastery of the medium.

Good quality paper is expensive and not easily found. Rising costs of production too often mean that the handmade sheet is not a viable proposition. I experience difficulty in finding a paper exactly suited to my own requirements, usually the sizing is not to my satisfaction. Many otherwise good papers I find to be too absorbent, and if one compares modern papers with the older paper used by Turner and his contemporaries, the old papers appear to have more 'body' and were more discreet in surface. I confess to finding many modern papers with their obvious textured surfaces so conducive to those sparkling 'watercolour effects' quite unsympathetic.

I have in my possession some Whatman paper (alas, no longer produced) watermarked 'Turkey Mill 1834'. It may well be worth more than the painting which goes on it! This has so fine a surface that the most subtle of nuances is legible and it will take strong colour without loss of saturation. I confess to a certain nostalgic glow of satisfaction when I reflect that this paper was made in the year that Turner made his watercolour studies of the burning of the Houses of Parliament, and that he may subsequently have used it.

The widespread use of cotton in paper manufacture nowadays does, I think, pose a problem. I have discovered that even if I stretch the paper before using it, it cockles again when it is re-wetted. I believe this to be the fault of the cotton.

Here is a list of some of the handmade and mould-made papers commonly found on the market nowadays. Paper makes have a habit of being discontinued, so check availability. I advise students to experiment with small quantities of a variety of papers in order to discover their characteristics.

Arches paper (French). Mould-made, Not and Rough, approximately 72–300 lb (150–635 gsm).

J. Barcham Green paper. Large range of watercolour papers in all surfaces, including Crisbrooke and De Wint papers.

Bockingford paper. Mould-made, Not, 90–140 lb (185–295 gsm). Very absorbent.

David Cox paper. A warm, oatmeal-coloured paper, similar to De Wint but less textured in surface.

De Wint paper. Not, 90 lb (185 gsm). Unbleached oatmeal-coloured paper, a modern imitation of a cheap wrapping paper which the painter Peter de Wint favoured.

C. M. Fabriano papers (Italian). Mould-made, Not, approximately 72–130 lb (150–165 gsm). The range includes some tinted papers.

Green's Pasteless Board. HP, Not and Rough, 200–400 lb (425–850 gms).

Hollingworth Kent Made Drawing paper. HP, Not, 40–130 lb (110–165 gsm). A high quality cartridge paper in several sizes up to 40 × 27 in. (1016 × 686 mm).

RWS paper. Handmade, HP, Not and Rough, 72–140 lb (150–295 gsm).

T. H. Saunders paper. Handmade and mould-made, HP, Not and Rough, 44–240 lb (135–535 gsm).

Tumba Ingres papers (French and Italian). 33 lb (104 gsm).

Plate 15 These much enlarged photographs of paper surfaces were taken in a 'raked' light in order to reveal the characteristics of their surfaces. Irregularities are of course much exaggerated.
a. J. Barcham Green Crisbrooke, Handmade Not 140 lb/295 gsm. The photograph reveals the coarse texture of this paper. The paper is tinted, a warm oatmeal colour. Notice the horizontal and diagonal markings of the mould. Useful for painters who like to work in a direct, bold style.

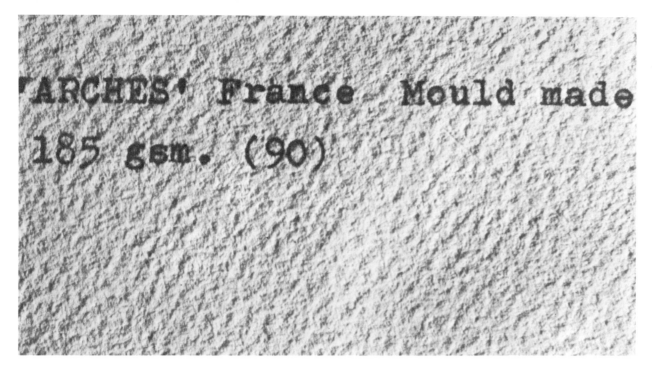

'ARCHES' France Mould made
185 gsm. (90)

b. Arches. Mould-made Not 90 lb/185 gsm.
   The mould-made papers have a more
   mechanical surface than the irregular,
   handmade papers. This photograph
   reveals a strong diagonal pattern. A good,
   stout, reliable paper which is very
   popular.
c. J. Barcham Green Cotman. Handmade
   Not 90 lb/185 gsm.
   This paper has a well balanced rather
   discreet surface and behaves well under
   repeated wettings. Recommended.

J.BARCHAM GREEN 'Cotman'
Hand made Not 90 lbs.

d. J. Barcham Green Hale Mill HP 90 lb/
185 gsm.
This paper has a softer, more glazed
texture than the other papers illustrated.
Hot-pressed papers, being smoother in
texture, are more favoured for body
colour and certain commercial uses.
This is a good white paper.

e. T. Hollingworth Kent Cartridge
90 lb/185 gsm.
This is a celebrated cartridge paper,
machine-made with a good, dense
mechanical surface, the evenness of
which can clearly be seen in this
photograph. Made principally for
drawing purposes, it is too bland for
most watercolour painters, but may be
used for more delicate *premier coup* work.

Here are three examples to illustrate further the effect that the texture of a paper has on the behaviour of the medium. These are very basic exercises indeed and yet they serve to show one of the most elementary principles of watercolour painting and should be studied carefully. The papers used are all 'Arches' mould made (French).

As a demonstration exercise I placed a small apple on a window ledge so that it was seen against a background of changing cloud forms and trees. One therefore had contrasting forms, soft and hard, amorphous and solid, linear and 'massy', light and dark, against which one could pit one's skills of drawing. Certain constants remained alongside the variables.

The object of the exercise was to demonstrate how these elements would be influenced by the paper surface. The exercises were not pushed very far and students should accept them only as models of similar exercises which they may devise for themselves.

f. Rough Not 140lb/300 gsm
The surface is extremely coarse and this gives the tones a 'jumpy' effect. There is a lot of fragmentation on these brush strokes and the more delicate passages have disappeared. This surface is suitable for heavy, unsubtle 'bravura' painting.

MATERIALS

g. Medium Not 72lb/153 gsm
Here the tones still have delicacy but they also have more 'bite'. The brush marks are evident but not hard: the surface of the paper is just rough enough to begin breaking up the paint at the end of the brush stroke. The dark of the sky is regular and control is relatively easy.

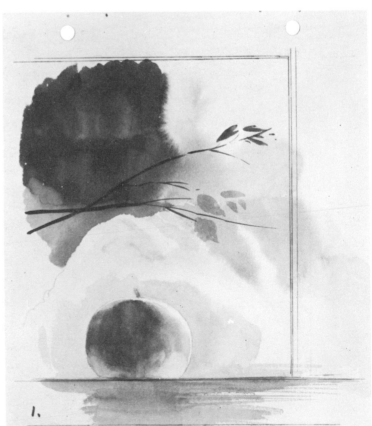

h. Smooth HP 72lb/153 gsm
Essentially a subtle paper, the tones are very soft and delicate. The dark tones are somewhat 'patchy' as the surface is very absorbent. The dark of the sky is irregular: control is very difficult without experience of the characteristics of this paper.

Practice of watercolour painting

Colour Plate 1 *The Sun breaking through Cloud* 1974. Watercolour $10\frac{1}{2} \times 14\frac{1}{2}$ in./ 266×368 mm. Collection Alan Smith, Epsom.

Colour Plate 2 *Jackdaws flying over the Sea* 1975. Watercolour 11 × 15¼ in./ 279 × 387 mm. Author's collection.

The storage and preparation of the paper. If you are anything like most painters in watercolour you will become very 'paper-conscious' and will take great pleasure in building up a stock of papers which you like to use. When you do so, give some consideration to the storage of the paper. Keep it flat, preferably in a large drawer, such as in a plan–chest, or failing this on a shelf at least as wide as the paper. If you cannot store it in a drawer keep it clean by covering with cheap plain paper—not newspaper, the print sometimes comes off. The two enemies of your paper are dust and damp. Wherever you choose to store it, ensure that it is clean and dry. Do not store it on its edge, for example in a port-folio, and do not keep it rolled up. Do not store it where direct sunlight can play on to it, and do not half-cover it, because if you keep it unused for some time, you may discover that the 'exposed' half has become warmer in colour. Good modern papers should be light-fast but it is not worth taking any chances.

In order to prepare the paper for painting, it will probably be advisable to 'stretch' it. The heavier papers may not require stretching but generally speaking if you are working on paper of 130 lb (165 gsm) or lighter it is better to stretch it.

Plate 16 The paper has been cut to size and immersed for a few minutes in a tray of water. The time required for soaking will depend on the weight of paper. The paper shown here is a 90 lb (185 gsm) Not surface; heavier papers need a longer period. It is now lifted out and surplus water allowed to drain off.

How to stretch paper. When paper is soaked the fibres expand as they absorb the water and then shrink as they dry out. If the edges are gummed down during the drying process, the paper will pull tight like a drumskin and when you come to paint on it, it will not cockle further.

Fill a large bath, tank, sink or suitable vessel with clean cold water, sufficient to immerse the paper in fully and large enough for the paper to lie flat in it without distorting its shape. Leave for a few minutes (heavier papers may require longer periods of soaking). Remove and gently shake off the surplus water. Lay the

27   MATERIALS

Plate 17 Lay on the drawing board, pulling out the corners gently between finger and thumb to assist the stretching. Leave for a few minutes before gumming down. The paper frequently goes on stretching for a while after it has been placed on the board. If this happens pull out the paper again to reduce the cockling.

paper flat on a clean drawing board. With a clean cloth or paper tissue mop up any excess water on the paper. Do this very carefully, on no account rub the paper or you will disturb the surface. Then leave the paper for a minute or two before gumming. The paper may continue to stretch while on the board. If this happens you will notice that the paper tends to furrow in one direction more than another. Lift the paper at one end and with your finger and thumb gently pull the paper out a little.

Take some gumstrip (adhesive-backed brown paper strip) of as good a quality as you can purchase. You will find the large better

Plate 18 Cut some lengths of gummed-paper strip, wet them and lay them around the edge, allowing approximately ½ in. (12 mm) overlap on the paper and a larger margin on the board. Smooth out flat with the aid of a sponge and set aside to dry.

quality rolls more satisfactory to use and more economical in practice. I buy a good wide one and slit each strip along its length, it goes twice as far this way. Wet the gumstrip, sufficiently, but not so much that you wash the gum off. Then with about one third of the width of the strip on the paper and the remaining two thirds on the board, gum down the paper all round, smoothing down with a cloth. Ensure that there is good contact along each edge.

Lay the board perfectly flat. Do not tilt it and do not attempt to speed up the process by drying out in front of a fire. If one part of the paper dries out faster it will shrink unevenly and lift off.

Some teachers advise sponging the face side of the paper instead of soaking it. I do not advise this because there is a real possibility that you will 'fur' up the surface and make it very unpleasant to paint on.

Paper traditionally has a 'right' and a 'wrong' side. The 'right' is the side with the watermark legible on it. With a little experience you will differentiate between the two surfaces. In actual practice you will find that it does not make much difference which side you use.

I like to prepare several boards at a time, if they are spare. The sight of those beautiful flat white surfaces, stretched like drumheads, waiting to be painted on, is very inspiring. What actually goes on to them is sometimes a sobering experience, but that is a different story. Incidentally, stretch your paper on a stout board, not hardboard or card. You would be surprised to see what some misguided students use.

Your paper is invitingly waiting for you but before we embark on the painting I am going to discuss the other materials.

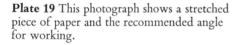

Plate 19 This photograph shows a stretched piece of paper and the recommended angle for working.

MATERIALS

Pigments

The modern manufacture of watercolour pigments involves somewhere between eighty and ninety colours (Winsor and Newton list). They range from a pale lemon yellow to ivory black, and in their scope offer the painter something in the region of seventeen yellows, twenty-one reds and oranges, ten greens, twenty blues and violets, fourteen browns, blacks and greys.

The standard of manufacture is extremely high and fortunately the range is so wide that the student of watercolour need have no fear that he or she will not be able to select a suitable range of colours.

The colours are made up essentially of transparent pigments which are ground to an exceptionally fine texture in an aqueous solution of gum. The proportions of pigment and binding agent are precisely combined to allow for the maximum variability of mixture, and dilution with water.

They must be capable of the most subtle washes and gradations without loss of colour content and must allow for extensive dispersal over the paper, absolutely evenly, with no spottiness or granular deposits. They must also allow for repeated washes to be placed one over the other without blackening, and must combine maximum strength (saturation) with translucency.

If one further considers that a colour may be required to function equally well in the Arctic Circle and in the Sudan, and that moreover no two painters will require precisely the same response from any one colour, then the high standard reached by the modern colourmen becomes evident.

There is a common misconception that watercolour pigments are more fugitive than oil colours, because they are exposed to light in thin washes on the paper. This is not true and although admittedly not all colours are equally durable, it makes no difference to their permanence whether they are ground into water or oil pigments.

Artists' colourmen like to classify their pigments in series of relative durability. For example Winsor and Newton classify their Artists' Watercolours in four degrees of permanence.

Class AA	Extremely permanent (24 colours)
Class A	Durable (47 colours)
Class B	Moderately durable (10 colours)
Class C	Fugitive (6 colours)

In all fairness it must be acknowledged that these terms are useful to the trade in defining degrees of permanence as a result of their ingredients or method of manufacture, but the terms are not absolute, and any subsequent test of durability in practice must depend on their use or misuse and subsequent exposure to light or atmospheric conditions. These colours are tested for their behaviour in a steady north light under glass and the testing does not involve extreme conditions. Most readers will be aware that in any case watercolour paintings should not be exposed to direct sunlight and that if they are framed the back of the frame should be sealed at the edges as a protection from damp or other injurious atmospheric effects.

From the foregoing colour classification you will notice that the majority come within the second category (Durable colours). This category presents the artist with the widest choice and given reasonable care the colours within it are perfectly reliable.

Watercolours are sold in two standards, 'Artists' and 'Students'. There is a wide difference between the two and although the latter may safely be used, the degree of strength and brilliance is by no means comparable. I advise students always to choose the 'Artists' range. They are admittedly more expensive but the extra money spent is well worthwhile.

You also have the choice of buying colours in whole pans, half-pans, cakes, or tubes of more than one size.

The whole pans are proportionately more economical to buy than the half-pans. They are convenient to use, offer a strong yield of colour wash and can be controlled easily where much dilution of colour is needed. This is what I use myself.

The tubes are more loosely ground, as is necessary in tube colours. They are useful if painters want a lot of colour at once and are not so subject to drying out because they can be resealed. I do not like them so much myself because of the 'runny' consistency, which I find difficult to control to the same degree.

Finally, cakes, the traditional form of watercolour, are composed of pure colour and yield pure unadulterated washes, but can go hard if not used frequently. They are still popular with the purists.

The choice of colour is, in the final analysis, a personal one, but allowing for this there are basic colours which most painters would agree are fundamental to a broad general range. These are listed below. The warm/cool distinction indicates whether a colour inclines to the orange or the blue end of the spectrum.

I am not suggesting that you use *all* these colours. They embody the main colour characteristics. A good basic palette for the beginner might consist of: raw sienna, light red, cadmium red, Winsor blue, alizarin crimson, sepia.

Learn to understand the potential of a simple range of colours to begin with, then gradually add one or two more colours to your palette. My palette at present is as follows, but I do not use all these colours all the time: aureolin—raw sienna—cadmium orange—vermilion—light red—cadmium red—scarlet lake—brown madder—alizarin crimson—rose doré—Winsor violet—Winsor blue—cobalt blue—Prussian blue—indigo—purple madder—sepia—Payne's grey—ivory black.

I sometimes include an olive green and a Winsor green, but because all greens have a tendency to a lack of density I seldom make use of them.

Although transparency is the prime factor governing the use of watercolour pigments, not all colours are equally transparent. For example, madders, lakes, cobalts and alizarins are naturally transparent, the cadmiums are not, but all can be used equally

Plate 20 Paints: Winsor & Newton tubes, half-pans, pans, cake.

MATERIALS

Colour family	Characteristics	
	Warm	Cool
YELLOW	cadmium yellow Indian yellow raw sienna	cadmium pale
RED	light red vermilion cadmium red	brown madder alizarin crimson
GREEN	olive green	viridian oxide of chromium
BLUE	Winsor blue (monastral blue) French ultramarine	Prussian blue indigo
VIOLET	mauve	Winsor violet
BROWN	warm sepia burnt umber	sepia

Auxiliary colour		
YELLOW		aureolin
ORANGE	chrome orange Winsor orange	
RED		rose madder
BLUE		cerulean

effectively if one is aware of the basic characteristics and one takes the appropriate action in using the colour. Equally, colours differ enormously in basic strengths of colour. Many modern synthetic colours composed of quinacridone or phthalocyanine have a strong staining capacity and need to be treated cautiously. However, half an hour spent painting out trial washes of each colour on paper, will soon acquaint you with the natural potential of each colour. I cannot go into great detail concerning the constituents of each colour, but listed in the bibliography at the end of this book there are some excellent sources of reference which will certainly provide all the information you may require.

Brushes

If it can be said that the paper on which one paints is the first factor conditioning the particular quality of the work produced, then the choice of brushes follows as a very close second.

All sorts of materials of course may be and have been used by painters in manipulating the colour washes on the paper: rags, mops, sponges, the painter's fingers, etc. I have used these materials myself where I thought the ends justified them, but the basic tool for the watercolourist is, of course, the brush. It is to the painter what the bow is to the violinist. It becomes an extension of himself and in practised hands is an instrument of infinitely subtle and precise inflexion, able to transmit to paper the finest shades of interpretation or emphasis.

Painters are usually pertinacious in their choice of a few brushes to which they have grown accustomed over the years. Peter de Wint painted much of his work with two, a thick stubby brush and one which was finer and which he teased out between finger and thumb to a sort of split end, used for painting foliage, etc. After a while, as a result of the use to which the brushes have been put, they take on a particular character, and would, in other hands, appear less sympathetic. This, of course, presupposes that the brushes are of sufficient quality to mature with use.

The art of brush manufacture is exacting and the cost of skilled labour and rare materials results in high cost for a good brush. Students should purchase the best quality they can afford. Don't economize on quality, it is cheaper in the long run to have a few very good brushes and to look after them well, this way they will repay you a thousandfold.

Types of brush. Unlike oil painting brushes, the watercolour brush has a short handle for ease of manipulation. It may be made of hair from any one of a number of sources.

Plate 21 Sable Brushes: Winsor & Newton series 7.

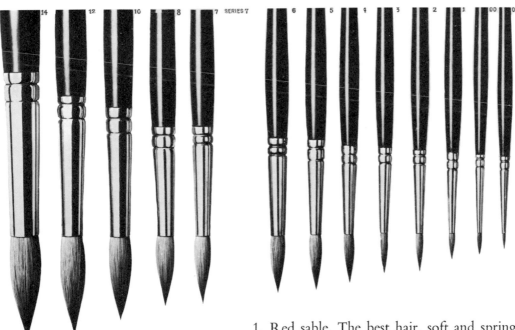

1. Red sable. The best hair, soft and springy and expensive. It has nothing to do with sable, but is made from the tail of the Kolinsky, a small rodent which is like a marten and is found on the borders of Russia and China.

Only the extreme tip of the tail of the animal is used in the best brushes. This is where the hairs naturally feather off to form a point. The process of manufacture involves a careful selection and grading of the hairs, which are laid all facing in the same direction and tied together in bunches, so that the longest hairs are in the centre and the shorter ones arranged in order round about. The brush is then fixed in the ferrule (the truncated cone which holds the hair) with a little glue.

This is necessarily a very brief and bald description of the skill involved in brush manufacture, which in the nimble fingers of the operatives takes only a few minutes to complete.

Apart from the pure red sable brushes, which are the best and most expensive, other grades or mixtures are used involving many animals, down to the cheap camel-hair brush, which has nothing to do with camels! In order of choice of selection the alternatives would run as follows:

2. Red sable and oxhair. The second most expensive variety, made from the ears of certain cattle combined with Kolinsky hair.
3. Oxhair. As above, made from hair from cattle ears; it is more springy than sable, and does not produce such a fine point, but because of its strength is preferred by some painters.
4. Squirrel hair. Relatively cheap brushes, possessing neither the spring nor the finesse of the other varieties.

There are other sources of hair used in brush manufacture, the origins of some being rather obscure.

The conventional range of sizes is from the minute 000 to size 14.

Chinese and Japanese brushes are popular and are easily obtainable. They are made with bamboo or reed handles and are, as one might expect, beautifully made. The long years of Oriental

Plate 22 *Break in the Clouds* 1974. Watercolour 19⅝ × 28⅝ in./499 × 727 mm. Author's collection.
This is one of a number of large studies made on the spot in winter. I had visited the Edvard Munch exhibition at the Hayward Gallery in London and had been particularly impressed with his direct landscape studies. Inspired by these I came home and carried some out myself.

Plate 23 *Blue Anchor Bay, Watchet* 1973.
Watercolour 14⅝ × 22¾ in./371 × 569 mm.
Collection Dr Tench, Florida.
Painted from studies made at Blue Anchor
Bay in North Somerset, looking towards
Minehead. The time is later afternoon, the
air is hot and oppressive, a heavy pall of
cloud hangs overhead, there is a threat of
thunder, A sea mist drifts inland over the
distant headland so that the further shoulder
and foot of the cliffs are lost to view. The
woods run down to the sea and the blunt
nose of the headland appears in silhouette.
The rocks in the foreground echo in reverse
the distant landscape.

This was painted sometime later in the
studio, on a 90 lb (185 gsm) Not surface
paper, using a reduced palette of sepia,
indigo, violet and a little raw sienna. The
distant headland was brushed into a
previously damped surface so that the tones
appear to emerge gradually.

tradition determine the character and use of these brushes and
they do not so readily adapt to Western modes of painting, but
are more nearly suited to the calligraphic style of painting for
which they were originally designed.

Some artists' or designers' brushes are set in quills. They come
in about six sizes from the equivalent of 00 to about 6, but are
classified under the romantic labels of : 'Lark', 'Crow', 'Duck',
'Large Duck', 'Goose' and 'Large Goose'.

Other variants which are obtainable on the market are square-
ended sable brushes, so-called wash or sky brushes, usually in my
estimation a euphemism, as they are too floppy to use successfully
on a wash or sky, and (probably more useful) varnish brushes—
broad and flat, which are popular with many painters. I also know
painters who swear by a shaving brush for covering large areas,
although I have not used one myself.

Selecting and caring for brushes. To repeat it is always worth
buying the best brush you can afford. At time of writing the
price of, for example, a no. 12 series 7 Winsor and Newton red
sable brush (one of the best on the market), is over £17. The
purchase of the best is no small item.

Whatever fortune, or lack of prudence, encourages you to buy,
choose it carefully. Ask the dealer to provide you with a glass of
water, dip the brush into it and give it just one vigorous shake
downwards. The hair should come to a perfect point at once. If
it does, buy it. If not, try another. In any case you will be grateful
for the glass of water when you learn the price of the brush!

If you can afford it, three brushes, say a no. 4, 6 and 10 or 12, will probably give you as wide a range as you will need. Look after your brushes! Don't scrub hard with them, unless you use a brush strong enough to withstand the treatment.

Don't leave them standing in a jar of water.

Don't leave them dirty when they are not in use.

Don't put them away in a brush container, box or drawer while they are still wet, or mildew will form.

Don't carry them about without protecting the ends.

Wash them out thoroughly with clean water after use. If a brush is badly discoloured you may use a little soap, but rinse it out thoroughly. Shape the brushes to a point again with your finger and thumb, or between your lips if the brush is clean. Lay them aside to dry naturally.

If you do this the brushes will give you years of faithful service and will take on their own character which you will learn to recognize and value.

If one may offer some advice, which Izaak Walton in his *Compleat Angler* intended for fishermen—'. . . treat him as if you loved him, that he may live the longer . . .'.

Other materials

Apart from the principal materials of watercolour painting, the paper, pigments and brushes, there are other auxiliary materials or aids which are well worth considering.

The requirements for working out of doors, in which portability is the first consideration, differ somewhat from those of the studio, and I will take them in that order.

Watercolour came into popularity originally when artists and amateurs of the art needed some method by which impressions and souvenirs of travel could be committed to paper, and from their need arose the growth and continued manufacture of the

Plate 24 Detail of worktop with watercolour equipment.

portable painting equipment, in which there seems to be no lack of interest. These are chiefly: boxes, brush-carriers, stools, easels and a few sundries.

The paint box. It would be possible to improvise a variety of receptacles for the colours, and mixing pans. However, I would recommend a modern watercolour box, which is convenient, light to carry and relatively cheap. There is a wide choice on the market, made by leading colourmen. They range from small sketching boxes holding a limited number of half-pans of colour, to very large and sophisticated ones. There are even handsome mahogany boxes, equipped with tubes, china pans, brushes and a separate palette.

Whatever you choose don't choose one that is too small. The sort that is most useful has large pans for mixing, offers scope for a dozen or so colours, if you need them, is robust and easy to clean.

I use one which is largish, has six mixing pans shaped like half an egg (these prevent colour from spilling over if one tilts it), two square flaps, a detachable colour tray and a further flat mixing tray at the bottom of the box. The box has a thumb-hole in it for ease of holding. It is a little on the heavy side, but this is more than compensated for by its robustness and good design.

Boards and sketching frames. There are a number of proprietary sketching frames on the market. They consist basically of a fibre or ply panel with detachable strips which may be clipped around the edge, securing the paper. They hold a piece of paper of approximately a Quarter Imperial size (11 × 15 in., 279 × 381 mm), and are light and easy to carry. I do not like them much because they offer little support when working. I prefer a larger drawing board, even if it is heavier to carry.

Stools. Sketching stools have been in use for generations now, if only as a tangible acknowledgement of Dr Johnson's dictum that 'God's greatest gift to Man was the ability to sit down.' This may be so, unfortunately I have found that sketching stools have a diabolical propensity to collapse beneath me, usually in the middle of some tricky sky-passage. They are usually too small and unstable, and it is hardly conducive to concentrated study to be required to poise oneself like a trick cyclist, or be ready at an instant to leap up suddenly at the first sign of collapse. If they don't then they will almost certainly cut off the circulation in one's thighs, so I've given them up. I prefer to stand at an easel, and if I am too enfeebled, I take a light aluminium chair in which I can sit with the sure confidence that I can remain in that state until I choose to move.

Easels. If stability is an important factor for a stool, it is certainly so for an easel. There are a number on the market, although few are designed with the watercolourist in mind. I use a dual purpose one, in which the main shaft can be swung over into a horizontal position, and with an adjustable block, will effectively hold a Half Imperial drawing board securely. It folds up to a reasonable size and is quite strong. It can be fitted with detachable metal spikes on the legs (the easel's, not yours) to drive into the ground, which prevents slipping. The standing position is by far the best, offering one more mobility and the opportunity of standing back from one's work when the need arises.

Sundry materials. A brush-carrier, a custom-made metal tube with a detachable cap, and containing a strip of flat metal, to hold the brushes and protect the tips, is useful. If you do not wish to buy this, a flat piece of board about two inches wide by a little more than the length of the longest brush, and with two rubber bands to hold the brushes in position, will prove a cheap substitute. Whatever you use for carrying your brushes, do not leave them longer than is absolutely necessary in the carrier if they are wet. Mildew will form on the brushes if you do this, and a metal carrier will soon become rusty.

This, together with a water pot, a supply of clean water, some paint rag, a sponge, knife and drawing materials, all held in a stout canvas bag or some sort of hold-all, will complete your equipment. You will very soon learn to spare yourself and select the minimum amount of tackle necessary for your operations, and to take those precautions against accident or human frailty which can easily beset one out of doors, and often not within easy reach of remedy.

If you are considering working in the landscape, plan the excursion in advance, and apart from being in possession of a crystal ball, weather forecast and a foreknowledge of the place in which you plan to work, do make certain that your materials are all prepared and as you would wish them to be.

Stretch your paper to the proportions you think you will need. Check that you have an adequate supply of fresh water, a spilled water jar in the heart of a deserted stretch of country is not a welcome occurrence. Paint rag and some tissues for mopping up you will find very useful. Having checked your equipment, don't forget yourself! Which is perhaps even more important. Although fortitude and a sometimes sublime disregard for the elements often distinguishes the landscape painter from his more frail associates,

Plate 25 Drawing of Epsom Downs under snow.

Plate 26 *Downs under Snow* 1973. Water-colour 18¾ × 23¼ in./476 × 596 mm. Collection Mitsubishi Company, Japan. This painting was based on some photographs which I took in 1973 (see also Plate 25). In any case I was familiar with the location, having drawn and painted it on numerous occasions. Under snow the landscape had taken on a curiously geometric aspect. The strong cold winds had swept the snow clear of the areas of tall grass, leaving the broad, curving and tapering shapes of the short grass patches. These, and the turning marks of the cars in the foreground, like lay-lines in ancient landscapes, looked like the marks of an enormous drawing. The sky was a gunmetal grey and the white areas of snow were left as virgin paper. Care was taken to key the painted areas as accurately as possible against the white paper. Sometimes a dry brush of colour was used and textural areas were considered particularly important.

you would be ill-advised to rely too much upon these undoubted virtues. You will not do your best work when you are frozen, wet or famished.

The most important item is adequate footwear, if you are well-shod you will more readily accept any other deprivation. Your clothing should be adequate for your protection and comfort but not too cumbersome. What you choose will depend upon your purse, your person and whatever vestiges of personal dignity you wish to preserve in the teeth of inclement elements or the curious stare of fellow travellers.

You will in time devise your own little dodges for your own comfort and convenience. I knew a painter who advised a pile of newspapers to stand on, and I have painted by the Thames at Windsor in the teeth of a stiff east wind in February with two hot-water bottles in the pockets of my duffle coat.

After discussing the rigours of working out of doors it will perhaps be a relief to consider the conditions necessary for working in the studio.

If you are fortunate enough to have a room which you can set aside as a studio this is fine, but other people less fortunate may have to make do with the occasional use of a room, or the end of the kitchen table, if the children are not using it for their homework!

It would be impossible to advise on all conditions under which students are obliged to work, apart from general considerations as to lighting, sufficient space and access to water, etc. Let me, therefore, mention the lighting conditions for working and pass on to discuss the provision of a studio situation to which we may all aspire, even if we do not as yet possess it.

A good steady daylight (coming from the left if you are right-handed, the right if you are left-handed) is desirable, so that your work is seen without variation of intensity or direction.

If you choose to work in artificial light, this requires some fore-thought. There are many types of lighting available, and you should choose the one that results in the least change from day-light. Modern tungsten lighting is warm, cosy and although designed for domestic comfort is unreliable for watercolour paint-ing. It heightens the intensity of the yellow/orange end of the spectrum and conversely appears to sharpen the blues. Reds appear more dense and 'toneless' under this light and darker colours soon lose light and appear to blacken.

The fluorescent lights available on the market are numerous and range from warm pink to yellow to cold blue/white. There are some euphemistically called 'Daylight', or 'Natural', but they are not really reliable.

I use a 40 watt 'colour matching' tube by Osram and I have found this over the years to be pretty satisfactory. No artificial light will be the equivalent of clear daylight. But this light, apart from a slight tendency to flatter by increasing colour contrast a little, is very reliable and the change from artificial light to day-light does not result in an anti-climax when one views the results on the following morning. The position of the tube is important.

Plate 27 Studio worktop.

THE PRACTICE OF WATERCOLOUR PAINTING

Do not put it too far from the work surface and place it so that you are not constantly casting a shadow over your work.

I prefer to work standing at a bench which is taller than the average table, being thirty-six inches high by thirty inches deep and quite long, stretching along one wall. My paper, mounts, etc., are stored on flat shelves beneath the bench.

When one paints with watercolour it is advisable to work with the board tilted at a moderate angle, about 30°. If it is more than this the colour will drain quickly to the base of the paper, if less you will not see it comfortably. I use a custom-made adjustable rack, which allows me to set it in one of three positions (see Plate 27). You may purchase a similar accessory or make your own. If all else fails, a thick book placed under the board will do.

Plate 28 Materials.

Apart from a jar or jars of clean water, and a plastic bowl of water to rinse the brushes from time to time, I have a number of plain white plates or saucers for mixing colour, if necessary, and a stock of rag for cleaning, wiping out, and other uses. This is essential. I also like to have a box of paper tissues nearby for general mopping-up operations, and for picking up excess water on the brush when working.

Setting out the work space before beginning is an important part of the operation. I like to clear the top, lay clean white paper on it and spread my colours and brushes out ready to hand. I fill the water jars and lay out my drawings or sketches which may provide the ideas and information for the work. I try to do this methodically and deliberately, it helps to settle my mind and concentrate my attention on the work and prepare myself for the job in hand. I don't think there is anything precious about this, it is a very necessary method of focusing attention. There is a description of an early Chinese painter who began work in a similar fashion, setting his table before the window, stretching out his silk, laying out his brushes and carefully preparing his inks before he began to paint.

Plate 29 *Coverack* 1971. Felt-tip pen drawing 4 × 5¼ in./102 × 133 mm.

Plate 30 *Coverack* 1971. Felt-tip pen drawing 4 × 5¼ in./102 × 133 mm.

Of all the visual arts, painting in watercolour is probably the most demanding in concentration. One needs to rehearse it in one's mind, endeavouring to envisage the complete idea before one begins and then to execute it clearly, swiftly and completely. This is very demanding and one doesn't always succeed. I am frequently quite nervous before I begin, almost like a musician before a concert, and will sometimes resort to any device to avoid that frightening moment when the first mark of colour goes down on that pristine white surface. After that the tension eases somewhat, and one is caught up in the struggle to control and develop the idea. But don't let me put you off. I only mention this to show that I have my misgivings too.

Colour Plate 3 *A Cornish Cottage* 1975.
Watercolour 13½ × 17 in./342 × 432 mm.
Private collection.

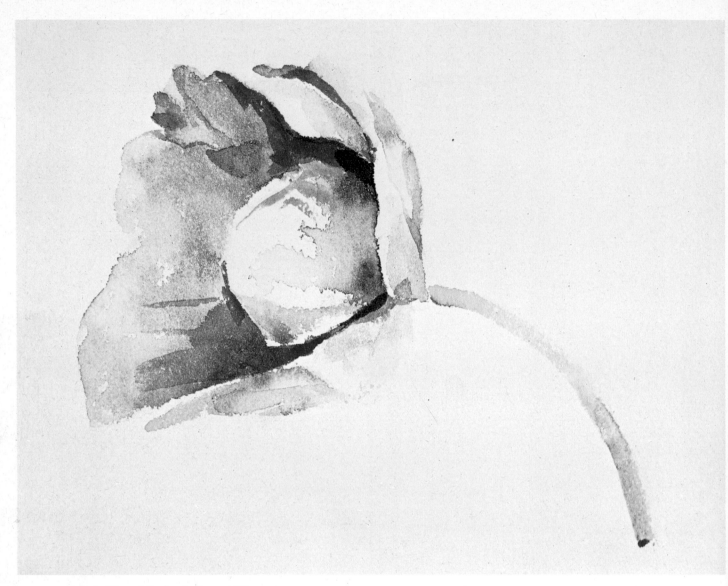

Colour Plate 4 *Study of a Poppy* 1974.
Watercolour 4 × 6 in./102 × 152 mm.
Author's collection.

3 Study:drawing

Treatises on education and methods of study have always appeared to me to have one general fault. They proceed upon a false supposition of life, as if we possessed not only a power over events and circumstances, but had a greater power over ourselves than I believe any one of us will be found to possess . . .

Sir Joshua Reynolds, *The Twelfth Discourse*, 10 December 1784.

Get a flat surface that won't crack,—some coloured substance that will stick upon it, and remain always of the colour it was when you put it on,—and a pig's bristle or two wedged in a stick; and if you can't paint, you are no painter; and had better not talk about the art.

John Ruskin

. . . I am often being asked by people, how does one set about writing a play? It is really very simple. If you have a feeling for it, you can. If you have not, you cannot . . .

George Bernard Shaw

I include the foregoing quotations in order to strike a cautionary note. The purpose of this book is to give to serious students information concerning the materials and practice of watercolour painting and to offer such advice on procedure as my experience allows me, in the hope that others may share my pleasure and understand their own problems the better.

But you cannot learn to paint in this or any other medium simply by reading about it. You may follow the most astute advice and copy the best examples of existing works, but in the end you must produce lots of watercolours, test out your progress in the light of your own experience, and, in spite of all your trials and disappointments, have a love of it at heart. If you have

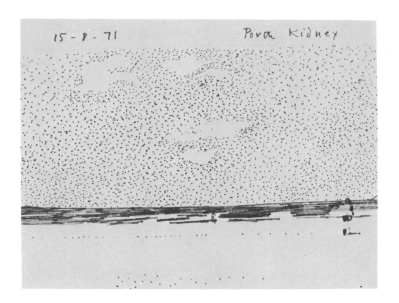

Plate 31 *Porth Kidney* 1971. Felt-tip pen drawing 4 × 5¼ in./102 × 133 mm.

this you will succeed; if you have not, an essential ingredient will be missing, however outwardly accomplished the work appears.

You must have a feeling for the medium; if you have it you won't need my advice. If you have not got it my advice will not provide it. Which pretty effectively, you may say, renders this book obsolete and is not calculated to boost the expectations of my publisher. However, in justification of all the hours spent in writing this, it is not quite as simple as that.

Feeling alone, however genuine, will not of itself produce good work, any more than a feeling for playing the piano will of itself produce a first-class musician. It has to be studied, worked upon and practised assiduously.

Unfortunately, watercolour has suffered by a sort of reverential isolation. It has been regarded as a specialist accomplishment, more akin to conjuring than to painting, and it is scarcely surprising that it has been seen by some as an anachronism. Watercolourists have at times unwittingly contributed to this misunderstanding by refusing to see it in a wider context.

If you are to succeed you must study all types and periods of art. Segovia has complained of many of his pupils, that they were not interested in music, only in the guitar, and I would paraphrase this by accusing many devotees of not being interested in art, only in watercolour. It is crucial that you study in a broad context. Go to galleries and museums and look at art of all schools and periods, ancient and modern. In so doing you will build up your critical powers and insight and will be the better able to evaluate your own progress, and lay the foundations of your own personal vision and character.

What should one study? This is perhaps the first question that the student is likely to ask, and the answer is not as simple as might at first appear. I think that whatever advice may be given it is necessary to point out that this is not binding in any absolute sense, but rather is offered as a broad structure or framework, within which there is a good deal of personal interpretation or emphasis which the student may, in his or her own wisdom, determine.

Assuming that one has sufficient basic materials of the sort already discussed, and that their reliability and suitability is not in question, then I think the order of study may be divided into three broad areas, within which further subdivisions may be made. These are:

1. Procedure. The study of the ordering of the activity.
2. Enquiry. The determination of the basic idea of subject, the visual analysis and translation of information.
3. Evaluation. The critical analysis of the subject and work and the measuring of one against the other.

Watercolour drawing differs in one respect from all other painting, in that colour and form are created spontaneously on paper with no subdivision of procedure and intention, and it is this ability to retain the idea and give it immediate expression on paper which is the determining characteristic of the watercolourist. It involves a highly concentrated activity over a comparatively short space of time, and I believe, although I cannot prove it, requires a particular temperament: the watercolourist

Plate 32 *Epsom Common* 1970. Pen and chalk drawing 11 × 14½ in./279 × 368 mm.

Plate 33 *Aysgarth Falls* 1971. Ballpoint pen drawing 4 × 5¼ in./102 × 133 mm.

must be imaginative, have a retentive memory, and be a sure executant.

For me drawing is the heart of the matter. By drawing I do not mean the meticulous description of a given situation or subject, but the rapid noting down of the elements of an idea, usually 'a visual experience', to impress them upon the memory before they vanish or are overlaid with secondary impressions.

The practice of drawing offers an activity and discipline which involves all the areas of mental activity, in particular memory, comprehension and assimilation, together with discipline of hand and eye. It lies at the very roots of our experience.

You must practise it constantly and assiduously. 'Draw everything and anything.' This was the advice given to Lucien Pissarro by his father Camille, and it still holds good today.

I would advise the student who has had no previous experience in using watercolour to begin by making lots of preparatory drawings, and even if he or she has had some previous experience, to maintain the practice of making drawings as the best

Plate 34 Study for *Jackdaws flying over the Sea* (Colour Plate 1) 1974. Felt-tip pen drawing 4 × 5¼ in./102 × 133 mm.

It is equally important in a so-called 'abstract' painting, whether the picture plane be uniformly on the surface, for example in a painting by Mondrian, or behind it, as in a work by Braque.

If you are dealing with landscape subjects, which is the main concern of watercolourists, then an awareness of values and their role in painting is critical. Generally speaking, values in the foreground of your subject will appear stronger and more sharply divided, and as you look back into the distance the values will be softer, less sharply divided and generally cooler in colour.

If you examine the *Mont Ste Victoire* by Cézanne reproduced in Plate 38, you will see an example of this principle at work. This drawing is one of several which Cézanne made of this subject. It dates from the last years of his life, and it is one of the greatest watercolours ever painted. It is a delight in its breadth and delicacy, and it exhibits that economy of expression which one might expect from a painter of great experience.

The delineation of the landscape features is spare but lucid. The colour values are confined to the shadow and middle areas of the forms, the right hand side of the forms is left blank and this is the side receiving the light, the sun is high up and to the right, the time about midday.

The whole is based upon a square frontal design, short squat trees mark the foreground and appear, singly or in groups, dotted across the parched plain to where the bleached form of the mountain, a great limestone outcrop, rises steeply in the distance, its southern face turned towards the sun and its long

STUDY: DRAWING

sloping saddle-back dropping away in violet shadow to the north.

The colour values in the foreground are tints of orange and emerald and violet and as one moves back into the picture they pass through sienna and grey to the pale limpid washes of blue and violet in the distance.

Tones do not so much depict the forms as gently caress them and merely infer their presence. They are more like stepping stones from one point to the next and, by a marvellous wit, the areas of white paper left between are not negative passages but serve to complement and link one subtle nuance of colour to the next.

When you have achieved a measure of confidence with your drawing practice and have exercised this by dealing with a variety of subjects and situations, in the studio and outside, turn your attention to the use of the brush and use it to cope with the matter of colour values.

I would urge you at this point to draw directly with the brush and, taking advantage of the lessons which may be learnt from the discussion of the Cézanne drawing, to endeavour to build up your own studies without recourse to preliminary drawing in pencil or other media. By so doing you will train yourself in control of the medium, and the ability to estimate values quickly and accurately.

Plate 39 *Peaches* 1974. Watercolour study 7 × 10½ in./178 × 267 mm.

Colour Plate 5 *A Rose* 1975. Watercolour
11½ × 15 in./285 × 381 mm. Private
collection.

Colour Plate 6 *Romantic Landscape* 1974.
Watercolour 11 × 14½/279 × 368 mm.
Author's collection.

Colour Plate 7 *Moon over a Lake* 1974.
Watercolour $10\frac{1}{2} \times 14\frac{1}{2}$ in./266 × 368 mm.
Author's collection.

Colour Plate 8 *The Black Boat* 1974.
Watercolour 10 × 13½ in./254 × 342 mm.

Whatever your taste or ambition may be for your future work, begin by relating your basic exercises and studies to a simple visual experience. The lessons learned by using your skills of discernment (recognition and evaluation of the tones seen before you) and the control of the brush and medium as a drawing instrument will be infinitely more profitable than those empty gestures too often recommended in instruction books, the random brush marks and crude overlays of colour which are designed to demonstrate colour transparency, etc. One might as well hit the keyboard with a hammer to demonstrate the obvious truth that a modicum of physical force is a prerequisite for producing a note in music. It is much more profitable to put your studies intelligently within a context against which you can measure your grasp of the problem.

Choose a subject or situation where the lighting is not confused or confusing, preferably a cross light which distinguishes values in measurable graduations of colour, and select a simple basic number of values which impinge on one another and in which you can determine some vestige of unity or harmony and balance of area to area. In other words concern yourself with design in your studies, execute the simple, uncomplex ideas well, try to see the subject as a whole, keep each part in balance with its neighbour. In this way, whatever you may lack in virtuosity or technical skill, your work will always be distinguished by qualities of vision which override these other less important (but, alas, more often sought after) qualities.

THE USES OF A SKETCHBOOK

Apart from the completed drawings produced in the studio, (or sometimes outside) and the studies of landscape so far discussed, I use sketchbooks a good deal. The whole idea of a sketchbook is that it should be a method of noting down a scene before you, and it should always be with you so that in any situation or at any time, you can take it out and make a drawing, or some notes, as a reference for your work.

Ideally, a sketchbook should be made of a cartridge paper, it should be well bound and be of a suitable size that will fit into a jacket pocket or a bag. The obvious point here is that you should be able to take it with you wherever you go. It is possible to buy sketchbooks of this sort although they are expensive. Of course, any notebook or booklet will suffice for making rough note-type drawings: the most important thing is always to have some book or booklet with you when you are suddenly confronted with a scene which you want to remember. Some of the best rough working drawings made by painters are done on the back of cigarette packets, and not necessarily in an expensive sketchbook.

The drawings and notes you make in a sketchbook can be done in any medium. Of course, pencil is best as it is the most

Belmont Hospital in distance:

Plate 40 *Belmont Hospital in distance.*
Watercolour $5\frac{7}{8} \times 8\frac{1}{4}$ in./148 × 210 mm.
A combination of linear brush drawing
and broad colour values, while the
drawings are economical, the values are as
accurate as possible. Author's collection.

versatile drawing instrument, but don't be afraid to use felt-tip pens, fountain pens or biros: the important point is to draw. If you make a point of taking your sketchbook with you at all times, no matter what your job or vocation, or how you fill your day, you will soon learn to take it out in a situation where you have five or ten minutes to spare and start to draw what is in front of you. This could be while waiting for a bus, while sitting in the back of a car on a journey, after a meal, and best of all when you are out walking in the country or on holiday. By making a habit of taking out your sketchbook and drawing whenever you have the chance during the day, you will soon develop your drawing ability and you will also begin to see with more discernment. To repeat the advice of Camille Pissarro, 'draw everything and anything'. By drawing as often as you can, no matter how quickly or sketchily, you will become much 'fitter' as an artist, and when you go out to paint a scene or a landscape in watercolour, you will find it much easier to start work, having practised drawing as much as you can every day. There is no substitute for working little and often.

Of course sketches will always be less full than studio paintings. The whole idea of a sketch is to try and capture the essential structure of a scene rather than the fine delicate details and tones. In trying to capture the structure of a scene, sketching will make you much more accomplished at understanding composition.

Plate 41 *Banstead Downs.* Watercolour
5⅞ × 8¼ in./148 × 210 mm. Author's
collection.

I use sketchbooks both as a means of collecting information and as a discipline to train my hand and eye. The main task I set myself is to set down the values and the basic fabric of the drawing as unequivocally as possible. Sketchbooks are a very good method of training and I thoroughly recommend you to have one with you at all times. It will help you develop your love of painting and drawing.

Plates 40–45 are six quick watercolour sketches taken from my most recent sketchbook. You can see that each one acts only as a set of notes for a painting, or as a small experiment in handling a certain cloud formation, or the way the evening sun softens the sky and casts a glow over what has been a brilliantly lit midday landscape.

Plate 42 *Rocks at Vellandreath*. Watercolour
$5\frac{7}{8} \times 8\frac{1}{4}$ in./148 × 210 mm. Author's
collection.
Painted early morning, the rocky outcrop
and the coastguard's hut below are in
shadow. The distant headland is pale in
the mist.

Plate 43 *Late afternoon—Sennen Cove.*
Watercolour 5⅞ × 8¼ in./148 × 210 mm.
Author's collection.

STUDY: DRAWING

Plate 44 *8.30 pm. 22/8/1976.* Watercolour
$5\frac{7}{8} \times 8\frac{1}{4}$ in./148 × 210 mm. Author's
collection.
Evening light—soft, melting colour values.

THE PRACTICE OF WATERCOLOUR PAINTING

Plate 45 *12.30 pm. 23/8/1976.* Watercolour
$5\frac{7}{8} \times 8\frac{1}{4}$ in./148 × 210 mm. Author's
collection.
Hot midday sun. Dark sea to right. On far
left a bank of sea-fog is moving up on
the horizon. A following wind from the
west opens a gap in the clouds.

STUDY: DRAWING

Dark olive green

Box Hill 4.00-5.00 pm. Thursday 8 June '72

Plate 46 *Box Hill 4.00–5.00 pm. Thursday 8 June 1972*. Pencil 9 × 10½ in./ 229 × 262 mm.
This drawing and the following were used as a basis for a large painting. This famous beauty spot has been drawn and painted by many artists. I was particularly concerned with the swelling contours of the hill and the way the trees embraced the southern slopes. Duration, approximately one hour.

I cannot over-emphasize the importance of drawing as a means of study, as it involves observation and understanding, if practised assiduously. It is sometimes a very good exercise for a watercolour painter to go out into the country with just drawing paper and pencil, and spend time simply drawing. This again heightens your perception and helps you with the construction of a painting.

There is a great difference between a sketchbook drawing, and a careful and well thought out study of a subject. A sketchbook drawing should be little more than a series of quick visual notes, whereas a full drawing can contain most of the work and solutions to problems for a painting that is to be done on your return to your studio.

When you go out with the sole purpose of drawing, it is a good idea to start by spending a short time in front of your subject in the way that you would do quick drawings in a sketchbook. You can increase the length of time as your experience and ability to concentrate grows, and correspondingly, your drawings will develop more fully. The most important point to remember when drawing is that you should never make a generalization or an empty gesture on the paper. Make every mark mean something and if you intend to put a line on the paper but haven't really thought what it represents, then leave it out. In this way you will develop an economy of style and a real strength in your line, and the marks that you do place on the paper will all have been carefully considered and they will all 'say' something.

Plate 47 *Box Hill 8/6/1972.* Pencil 9 × 10¼ in./229 × 260 mm. The second version was quicker and the concentration more upon the rhythmic flow of the clumps of trees at the foot of the hill.

STUDY: DRAWING

Plate 48 *Crackington Haven*. Pencil
7¼ × 11 in./184 × 280 mm. This narrow
inlet on the North Cornish coast is dramatic, the rocks and high cliffs have been
scooped out in long flowing ridges by
the Atlantic rollers. Study for a painting.

Plate 49 *Fog in Burgh Heath Road—November*
Pencil 7¼ × 11 in./184 × 280 mm.
Drawn from the kitchen window. The
houses in the road are almost invisible
and the lines of the lime trees and the
polygonum creeper make a delicate tracery
against the yellow sky.

Plate 50 *Hawk among the house-martins.*
Pencil 7¼ × 11 in./184 × 280 mm.
Drawn in the garden one late summer
evening. The house-martins were swooping
over the trees and were apparently
unperturbed by the kestrel which suddenly
appeared in their midst.

STUDY: DRAWING

Plate 51 *Downs under snow I*. Pen and sepia ink 10 × 14 in./254 × 355 mm. A freezing day under a sky like a leaden sheet. The conditions necessitated rapid execution. I used a steel pen and my finger tips dipped into the ink. A piece of rag served to wipe in the sky and foreground tones.

Plate 52 *Downs under snow II*. Pen and
sepia ink 10 × 14 in./254 × 355 mm.
The light had almost gone by the time
I began the second drawing. The wood
pigeons fly off to roost in the nearby woods.

Downs under snow II.

STUDY: DRAWING

Plate 53 *Bracken Path—Epsom Common,
Tuesday 6 January 1970*. Pen, ink and watercolour 10 × 14 in./254 × 355 mm.
It was a bright afternoon in January when
I made this drawing. The winter sunlight
had already begun to thaw the recently
fallen snow. The drawing is more of an
information sheet than a record of a particular place. The written notes, intended
as a support to the drawing, serve to
amplify the memory of the situation.

Plate 54 *The Magpie*. Pencil and chalk
10¾ × 14½ in./273 × 292 mm.
This served as a study for a watercolour
which follows the drawing faithfully.
The magpie flew over as I was drawing
and I incorporated it.

INTERPRETATION

What attracts us to particular subjects is essentially a mystery, but apart from purely 'subjective' influences (for example, a thatched cottage is *ipso facto* a more rewarding subject than a council house, which probably has more to do with nostalgia than perception), there are usually other aspects of which one may be dimly aware: for example, a quality of lighting, a unity of colour, contrast of texture. If you recognize the source of the initial attraction, endeavour to keep this dominating aspect in the forefront of your intentions so that all your ploys are directed to this end.

In beginning to draw directly with the brush, the student should first of all concentrate on the visual analysis of the subject, that is upon the relationships that exist between one area and another, between one value and the next. It may for example, be between the edge of a belt of trees and the sky beyond in a landscape, or the turn of an apple in shadow against the tablecloth, as in a still life, or any number of comparable situations, and in all of these, endeavour to state values of colour as directly and unequivocally as possible.

When you have practised painting directly in this manner, you may turn your attention to the question of brush control.

STUDY: DRAWING

Plate 55 *Birling Gap* 1971. Watercolour study 7 × 10 in./178 × 254 mm.

We don't know precisely who invented the brush, the Chinese were using them in 3,000 B.C., and Egyptians used crude 'brushes' made from the crushed ends of reeds. Obviously at some point it was discovered that hair or bristles tied to a stick, for ease of handling, afforded a very convenient method of picking up and retaining small quantities of liquid and transferring them to a surface in a variety of marks; and it would seem that no amount of modern technology has been able to improve upon the basic efficiency of this tool. It is capable of the crudest or the most exquisite methods of handling and it would repay us to give a little thought to its uses.

Initially students encounter considerable difficulty over the estimation of water content to pigment held in the brush, so that one usually finds the brushwork either arid and mean in execution, or too wet, loose and vapid in colour strength.

While acknowledging the fact that generalizations can often be misleading, I tend to subscribe to the opinion that it is better to begin dryish and with experience build up a more fluid method of handling. One needs only that minimum of water in the brush which allows one to put down a value without patchiness; any excess over and above this is superfluous and will make control very difficult.

Bearing this in mind, endeavour to make your brush marks as

expressive as possible, watching how in order to portray the subject sometimes the colour needs to be thin, spare and transparent, at other times dense and opaque, or fluid areas of colour may be interspersed by dragged strokes of colour. Broad brush strokes, with the brush pinched out between finger and thumb, produce a mark quite unlike the same brush charged with full colour, and again firm pressure with the heel of the brush may be just right for some passages, at other times the fine point must be used. The secret is to be aware of all this and to do it without declining into flashiness of technique.

I think the distinguishing characteristics of the great draughtsman are restraint and lucidity, the ability to make the mark say precisely what it was meant to say, neither more nor less. This is very difficult. I have sometimes tried to copy brush drawings by Rembrandt (Plates 56, 57). It is a sobering and salutary experience, every mark expresses exactly what was intended, even down to the slightest rub. You could do worse than copy some of these drawings.

The effortlessness and artlessness of a drawing by Claude Lorraine, for example, or that of a modern painter like Dufy, is incredibly difficult. I should like someone looking at my paintings to snort and say 'I think my six-year-old could do that.' I should feel then that I had succeeded!

Plate 56 Study from Rembrandt drawing 1969. Pen and wash 11 × 14½ in./279 × 368 mm.

If you paint into a dry surface the brush strokes will remain separate and detached. If you paint into a damp or wet surface the brush strokes will fuse into the surface and will appear to lie below the surface. So in addition to the changing emphasis of execution just described, you have this other potential, unique to watercolour, the exploitation of its 'wetness'. You will need to experiment a good deal before you are able to use the whole expressive range of this potential—it is full of pitfalls for the impulsive and the unwary and can be very frustrating. You will need to be able to judge to a nicety the volume of colour to water or you will simply achieve great vapid areas of insipidity.

The chief quality of the 'wetness' of watercolour (which is after all an illusion) is its fluidity and mobility, resulting in the power to express suspended movement discussed earlier. Coupled with this is the attendant characteristic of transparency, the capacity to permit light reflection to pass through veils of colour with more or less intensity. This may be given full rein as in some of Turner's late watercolours, or slowed down to deep obfuscations of colour as in some of Blake's drawings.

Plate 57 Study from Rembrandt drawing 1969. Pen and wash 11 × 14½ in./279 × 368 mm.

Plate 58 J. M. W. Turner. *A Raft and a Rowing Boat on a Lake by Moonlight* 1840(?) Watercolour 7½ × 11 in./192 × 279 mm. British Museum, London.
This drawing may have been done in Venice or on a visit to the Swiss lakes. It is difficult to be certain about its origin and the date is conjectural. The subject would preclude painting on the spot and it was probably painted from pencil notes. It is built up with overlaid washes, sometimes painting into a wet area, as in the cloud passage where the moon breaks through, or hatching into dry areas as in the central areas surrounding the raft. Some body colour appears in the moon, and it may have been used in the central light area, though I rather doubt it. It combines powerful brush drawing and passages of infinite delicacy.

What we have here are the elements of a very powerful and beautiful medium, which, working within a narrow compass, is capable of wide dramatic and lyrical expression. Strange and sad therefore that such diversity of true colour and modulation should be so misunderstood by many people, for whom it is no more than a charming, if insipid, vehicle of outworn felicities.

4 Study: landscape

Constable pointed to a copy of a small evening winter-
piece by Ruysdael. 'This picture' he said 'represents an
approaching thaw. The ground is covered with snow, and
the trees are still white; but there are two windmills
near the centre; the one has the sails furled and is turned
in the position from which the wind blew when the mill
left off work, the other has the canvas on the poles and is
turned another way, which indicates a change in the
wind; the clouds are opening in that direction, which
appears by the glow in the sky to be the south (the sun's
winter habitation in our hemisphere) and this will produce
a thaw before the morning. . . .'

John Constable, The Third Lecture at the
Royal Institution, 9 June 1836.

Not only how far away, but the way that you say it
Is very important. Perhaps you may never get
The knack of judging a distance, but at least you know
How to report on a landscape: the central sector,
The right of arc and that, which we had last Tuesday,
And at least you know . . .

Henry Reed. Judging Distances from
Lessons of the War, 1914.

It is probably safe to assume that ninety-five per cent of the watercolour enthusiasts practising at any time are painting landscapes.
This is such a truism that even to draw attention to the fact
may provoke some perplexity. 'After all,' you will say 'so what?'
Nothing really, I suppose, except that since the rise of the
medium's popularity in Europe, particularly in England, during
the eighteenth century, our attitudes towards Nature and natural
landscape have found so eloquent an expression of its moods in
the use of watercolour, that in most minds they are inseparably
identified one with the other. There is something peculiarly

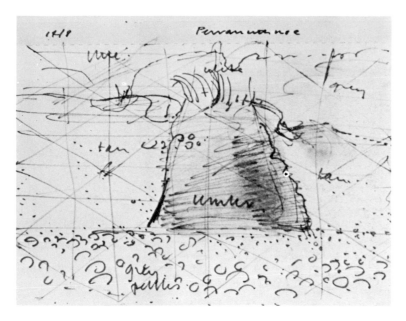

Plate 59 Sketch for *A Cornish Beach* 1969.
Pencil 4 × 5¼ in./102 × 133 mm.

Plate 60 *A Cornish Beach* 1969. Watercolour
10½ × 14½ in./267 × 368 mm. Author's
collection.

This grew from a drawing of a rock face on
a beach in South Cornwall (Plate 59), and
was built up rather slowly over a period of
some months, with several revisions. The
rock surface to the left at the back was
painted from a small piece of limestone
which I had in the studio. After all, one
cannot invent a rock—better to borrow one.
The sky is a deep blue to indigo (Winsor
blue and indigo), the rock face stone colour
to copper. There are deep madder shadows
to the right cooling to turquoise in the right
foreground. The boat is ochre and violet
and blue in the shadow, and the central
dark section in the background is umber and
dark sandalwood colour. A light warm
base colour was taken all over the paper in
the first instance, ignoring local areas. This
was modified as I progressed across the
paper—the colour shifted in the beach to a
silvery-cool blue in the immediate
foreground. The initial concern was to
create a balance by strong complementaries
as a basic framework of colour in which the
smaller, more specific areas of colour would
find their proper place. Eventually the
forms of boat, beach flotsam, etc., were
given clear definition.

STUDY: LANDSCAPE

Plate 61 *The Beach at Eastbourne* 1971.
Watercolour study 7 × 10 in./178 ×
254 mm.

appropriate in the way in which limpid washes of colour of
changing density, interspersed with sharper accents of solid
shapes, parallel the behaviour of light, gentle, shifting, diverse,
at times obscuring the forms of landscape and at other times
revealing a changing pattern of lines and shapes which give
identity and meaning to our visual experience.

I would like to say something about landscape painting and the
role of watercolour in the depicting of it, and in particular my
own approach to this subject.

Two quotations preface this chapter. They are very different
in form and essence, yet they have something, or rather several
things, in common.

I wonder if I had appended no names whether you would,
reading them for the first time, have recognized the authors?
They are separated by a distance of seventy-eight years—years
in which the most astonishing advances in industrial and socio-
logical change had taken place. They both exhibit a curious
detachment, one in an earnestness for precise information, the
other in an indifference to the nostalgic associations of landscape
which has now become the theatre of bitter struggle.

One could have been written by a farmer, the other by a sur-
veyor, instead of a painter and a poet. They are both charac-
terized by a concern for objective statement and an economy of

expression and therefore suggest an approach to the art of landscape which is cool but at the same time obsessive and penetrating. Three characteristics are exemplified in both, accuracy, economy and lucidity. I think these three should be the cardinal virtues to strive for in our watercolour studies, and they can only spring from an awareness of the nature of the subject, which in turn depends upon, first, the prevailing conditions at the time and, second, our attitude towards them.

'. . . that least interesting of subjects, the tame delineation of a given scene.' (Henry Fuseli).

Although my work has ranged over a number of fields, as far as watercolour is concerned it is rooted in the study of landscape, and it may be of some interest to discuss in more detail my own particular approach and methods of working.

On reflection it falls into two main categories: landscapes or work having a landscape basis which is essentially built up from notes and sketches in the studio; and landscapes painted directly on the spot. I have chosen two paintings which exemplify these approaches and what follows in photographic form is a stage by stage record of the building up of a painting. I hope the photographs will be sufficiently instructive to indicate this and that together with the text and captions they will illustrate a certain procedure. There are many ways of working and I do not assume for one instant that this is the only way. It seems to work for me because I am interested in certain aspects. I hope that it may prove helpful to students who have had little experience.

LANDSCAPE AT SENNEN COVE

This work was done with the aid of one or two studies made on the spot, but chiefly from memory and by a free interpretation of the material. My chief purpose was to establish a mood, and while I was not wilfully doing an injustice to the topographical features of the place, I was nevertheless more concerned with effects of light and weather at a particular time than with the accuracy of every geographical feature.

One of the delightful things about painting is that it is possible to bring together in the one work appropriate experiences that may not occur time-wise at once, but whose correspondence nevertheless has a quality of relevance which is more than mere verisimilitude. It is important to be aware of the spirit of the place. Whatever role we ascribe to imagination or vision this must be related to awareness, and I certainly consider a very critical sense of observation a prerequisite for my personal statement.

To set the scene, the place is Sennen Cove in Whitesand Bay, just north of Land's End and at the extreme westerly tip of Cornwall. The time, towards the end of August 1975, early afternoon. It has been raining and although there is a hazy light overall, soft rain clouds are drifting across the headland, which stretches in a long shoulder westwards, about half a mile to a mile away. The sea is quiet, of a deep indigo to gunmetal blue-grey, and a short distance away a woman and child are walking towards us through the tall marram grasses that top the dunes and partially obscure their figures silhouetted darkly against the afternoon light. Colours are subdued and fall within the two complementaries yellow and blue. Not obviously so. The colour falls into a sienna–sepia–madder on the warm side, and a grey-blue, indigo on the cool.

The overall light is soft, more of yellow-grey haze with the sun trying to come through. It is this ambience of light which one must endeavour to sustain, and all the other visual information must be subordinated to this overriding factor.

I have one or two sketches in colour, notes that have been made on the spot, I have drawings in sketchbooks, not necessarily of this precise situation but related in time and place, and I have memories of the place. Frequently the drawings may be mere shorthand jottings which serve to trigger off a memory of a situation and this is enough to go on. I find that too much information will obliterate my ideas by overlaying them with superfluous facts which I cannot use, and often I have preferred a slight drawing to an elaborate photograph, which seemingly offers more. I value the detached view, life seen out of the corner of one's eye.

So the few notes which I have and my memories of the place are all the evidence of study at my disposal and I try to work from this. I am now over three hundred miles away from the scene, in my studio, and four and a half months later anyway.

The paper is stretched, it measures about $11 \times 14\frac{1}{2}$ in. (279×368 mm). It is not ideal but it may serve as a study, if I do not try to be over-ambitious with it.

I do no drawing whatsoever on the paper. I endeavour to form

Plates 62–68 *Landscape at Sennen Cove.*
A restricted palette of raw sienna, madder lake, indigo and sepia was used throughout the painting. The paper used was lightweight, 72 lb (150 gsm), Hot-pressed and smooth. Not my favourite paper, and I did not like it much. It was only responsive to a continuously damp surface which had a tendency to cockle in spite of preliminary stretching. Tonality was difficult to control and dark accents tended to appear unsympathetic and 'jumpy'. Repeated overpainting was not practical in a paper of this weight and texture. The brush used was a Winsor & Newton series 7 no. 12 sable, except for one or two sharp accents in the foreground, for which I used a no. 6 sable of the same series.

Plate 62 The paper is damped lightly with a sponge before work is begun, and the soft banks of rain cloud are brushed in while the paper is still wet. The colour of the sky (sepia with a little sienna) is allowed to drift down, but lifting out towards the foreground.

THE PRACTICE OF WATERCOLOUR PAINTING

a picture in my mind of what the painting will eventually look like, rather more to establish a procedure for working than to delude myself into thinking that I can somehow forecast the result accurately. General proportions, estimated range of colour, broad elements of design—these are the essential ingredients which I try to think about at this time. This will allow for the things that cannot be foreseen to be recognized when they arrive in the work and, hopefully, to be assimilated into the scheme of things.

I damp the surface of the paper to prepare for those soft rain clouds and apply the first charge of colour to the paper. What follows is set out in photographs and attendant notes.

Plate 63 When the sky is dry a dark note is added on the headland and soft foreground tones are brushed in to represent the mist-bound slopes of marram grass above the shore.

Plate 64 The dark accent on the headland is damped slightly with a sponge and the receding tones of the land mass brushed in, working towards the distant coastline, modulating the values to describe the gently rolling contours.

STUDY: LANDSCAPE

Plate 65 The area of the sea has been damped and before it is quite dry a dark band of indigo colour is swiftly brushed on, beginning with a dark accent inshore and lifting off slightly to the right. The swiftness of the stroke is important and as you will see its momentum carries beyond the edge of the paper. Note that it will dry out lighter than it appears at this stage. It is important to be able to judge the anticipated loss of tone in drying.

Plate 66 The surface of the sea is now being worked on, the dark colour being allowed to soften as it descends the paper. Some darker accents near the edge of the shore are being added.

Plate 67 The area representing the dunes on the left is damped lightly with a sponge before the foreground accents are added. This is to make them sit back into the landscape and not merely appear on the surface. Further modification of tones in the left middle distance suggests light breaking over the horizon.

Plate 68 The study almost complete, the
little figures of a woman and child are
added, care again being taken to make them
sit back in the landscape. It is important at
this stage to look over the whole of the
painting and to add accent where necessary,
or subdue passages that appear out of key.

Plates 69–80 *Landscape on the Downs.*

Plate 69a Looking north from the Downs (facing left).

LANDSCAPE ON THE DOWNS

The study of the Sennen Cove painting relates to a landscape subject removed in time and place and built up in the quiet detachment of the studio with notes and drawings as *aides-mémoire*. This section of the chapter is concerned with a landscape painted on the spot and contains a photographic record of the situation and my approach to it.

I will try to set the scene as faithfully as I can so that students can relate the procedure to the subject.

The place: Epsom Downs in Surrey, looking north over Epsom a mile or so away, and over the broad flat plain of the Thames valley to London some sixteen miles away. The Downs is a long chalk shoulder at this point, nearly 500 feet above sea-level. A golf-course runs across the foreground and strangely garbed figures are dragging little trolleys of clubs behind them, stopping now and again to whack the white ball ahead of them, in what appears to me, almost totally ignorant of the game, a curiously random fashion. I am reminded of Benny Green's observation that he thought golf spoilt a nice walk! Occasionally a whirring sound overhead and a sharp thud as a ball comes uncomfortably

Plate 69b Looking north from the Downs (facing right).

close and lands in the long parched grasses nearby jerks me out of my thoughts but I take some comfort in the hope that I am a little too far off course for the muscular amateur, and the searing east wind will carry the balls away from me. I step back a little nearer the shelter of the hawthorn copse and endeavour to size up the situation.

The time: eleven o'clock in the morning of Saturday March 6 1976.

The conditions: it is the last day of a week in which we enjoyed cloudless skies every day, but in spite of the sun there is a cruel east wind sweeping over the Downs, bringing a threat of sleet or snow to follow, and making my eyes smart with the cold. Visibility is good but the edge of London is lost in a blue haze. Bands of distant blue trees intersect the landscape beyond the town; nearer, the trees appear dun coloured, with violet shadows. Here and there a tall building or hospital chimney punctuates the landscape.

The sun is behind me and I throw a long shadow on the grass. I examine the prospect through a radius of almost 180°. To the left and westerly a faint gleam of silver indicates the Thames near

Plate 70 Arriving at the scene, examining the view.

Staines; here the colour is ashen and cold. To the right and easterly the colour is fractionally warmer and an almost imperceptible pall of winter hangs over the city. I am aware of it out of the corner of my eye when I look straight ahead, but facing in that direction, screwing up my eyes against the glare, I cannot quite detect it.

Overhead the sky is a clear opalescent blue but becomes warmer and greyer with lilac opacity towards the horizon. As I let my glance drop down and forward to the foreground, the cool bands of blue and grey give way to umber and sienna. The colour shifts from cool to warm, top to bottom and, less so, west to east (left to right).

Ahead on the central axis the colour appears neutral and I cannot determine it. On the edge of the town a row of new houses show off their roofs like burnished copper. Half a mile away, in a paddock, tiny racehorses rotate slowly like a toy roundabout.

I walk up and down, crossing and re-crossing in front of the subject, looking for a natural balance until I think I've got the feel of it, and my impressions are beginning to crystallize. I make one or two notes in a small sketchbook. From my chosen pitch, determined by a compromise between my two conflicting desires, to obtain at once the best view and the maximum amount of shelter from that murderous east wind, I notice that the ground slopes down towards the centre both left and right, its line of descent marked on the left by the thin orange line of a sandy track, and on the right by a low-cut hedge that bounds a field. In the centre a tall clump of pines forms a natural pivot.

In contrast to the blue sky overhead, the ground in the foreground and near distance is a sienna colour, nearing ashen in the sparse hollows of the Downs.

The wind blows the tall yellow grasses in front of me; it reminds me of a Japanese poem:

> The Autumn wind
> In the dry grasses
> Scatters the dew
> Like a broken necklace.

Some large crows, jet black with ruffled feathers and clown faces, stagger about in the foreground.

I settle the limits of the painting and the placing of the horizon on the paper. I use a soft sponge charged with clear water to wet the paper in advance, a necessary precaution considering the drying conditions of combined sun and wind.

The paper is a 90 lb (185 gsm) Not surface RWS paper, stout and discreet in surface. It should prove docile enough in these trying conditions.

The colours I shall use will be raw sienna, light red, sepia, Winsor violet, Winsor blue, indigo.

Before I start painting, I try to get the main features of the landscape clear in my mind. I know that if I do not do this it will be too late once I have embarked on the paper.

Plate 71 Having settled on the position, I am 'framing up' the chosen section with my hands, to establish an approximate limit to the view.

This is done by looking at the landscape for several minutes before painting, letting it soak in, as it were. Gradually a sort of order establishes itself, whether this exists in Nature or is one we superimpose I would not like to say. I become aware of a scheme, the range of colour basically being blue v. yellow, with small touches of red—but all very subtle, in fact it is the hair-breadth subtlety of the values that I find interesting. The colours occur within a narrow band, the sky being fractionally lower in key than the ground, and through the middle distance brushed tones of umber and blue-grey.

81

Plate 72 Making some notes in a sketchbook, in order to sort out basic proportions.

At the same time I decide the placing of the horizon. This is the most important division. The proportion of sky to ground will determine the dramatic character of the landscape. I decide that there should be more sky than ground, and that the dark accents of trees, etc., should be near the centre. A group of pines marks the spot, in front of this to the left a larger soft mass of bushes just knocks the design off the symmetrical, making it more interesting.

From the photographs you will notice that the drawing board is tilted at a gentle angle. This is determined by one's own height, direction of light and so on. It would be difficult to see it comfortably if it were quite horizontal and equally difficult to control if the board was too steep. After all, the law of gravity plays a

Plate 73 The easel is set in position. I am about to make a pencil mark on the paper to establish the depth of the horizon. No more preliminary drawing than this was necessary.

Plate 74 Beginning at top centre the sky wash is put in, the colour modulating as the wash descends.

Plate 75 The initial wash almost complete, some indication of deepening tones in middle distance, the belt of trees in the centre and foreground tones are tentatively stated.

large part in watercolour painting, with the washes running towards the bottom of the paper.

I balance the water pot precariously on the extended arm of the easel, which admittedly is inviting disaster, and I should devise some safer method of securing it, although I will confess to only one accident in the past twenty odd years and that produced effects in the sky that defied description!

Using a mixture of Winsor blue and indigo I begin at the top centre of the paper and work sideways and downwards, adjusting the colour as I go.

Towards the horizon the colour becomes more ashen and slightly opaque. I have found that a little Chinese white—an almost imperceptible amount—is useful in order to introduce a hint of opacity into the distance.

The distance and middle distance is hazy. There are running across the landscape soft bands of blue-grey which melt into one another. They probably represent lines of trees and houses and are anything up to seven or eight miles distant and impossible to distinguish at this range.

As the tones melt into one another, I keep the paper slightly damp and paint into it. The object is gradually to bring the tones up to the foreground, increasing in strength as one goes. As the change is very gradual and nothing is exceptionally dark it is a very delicate operation. Too much contrast and it will look 'jumpy' or 'spotty', too little and it will appear flat and lifeless.

The darker accents of the trees are put in when the paper is covered and the overall mood of the painting established. Sometimes holding up a dark object against the landscape will be a help in judging the degree of change in the tone values. (In one of the photographs I am holding a black brush-carrier against the landscape.)

Plate 76 Having reached the end of the first stage, I am holding a black brush-carrier against the landscape in order better to estimate the tone values of the middle distance.

Plate 77 The paper has now been covered and the foreground colour values are strengthened. Note how, in spite of having been stretched, the paper cockles in long vertical furrows; these will pull out.

From now onwards, the key of the painting having been established, it is a question of introducing a little more information into the relevant passages and the accents of interest which give life and scale to the work.

I have been working for an hour or two on the painting by this time. A rather tattered gardening glove protects my left hand, holding the palette, from the cold wind; but my right hand is becoming very cold and I have difficulty in holding the brush, so it is time I stopped. I plan to return again when the conditions are similar enough to allow continuing with the painting.

The weather became increasingly cold and grey after this and it was not until a fortnight later, Saturday March 20, that I was able to return.

10.30 a.m. The same spot on Epsom Downs, looking north. A beautiful fine morning. There is still an easterly wind blowing but it is a little warmer.

The life around me is still exactly the same. The golfers are trailing across the course; riders on horseback emerge from the thickets and pathways. The crows are scavenging in the waste-

Plate 78 The paper has pressed out in drying, and working through the middle distance I am now strengthening and building up the tones.

paper basket and in the distance the racehorses are circulating again in the paddock.

As a result of the reduced wind visibility is reduced; there is a clouded look about the middle distance and many of the land-marks are lost to view. I decide to capitalize on the change and accept the simplified character of the landscape.

Plate 79 *Landscape on the Downs* detail.

THE PRACTICE OF WATERCOLOUR PAINTING

It is even more subtle now and every additional accent jumps from the paper. I have to damp each area before painting so that the values fuse into one another.

The paper is not responding too well. Repeated wettings followed by applications of colour deaden the surface. Unfortunately, the continued effects of sun and wind make this a necessary operation and as I work over the painting progress becomes more difficult. I long for the settled atmosphere of the studio where at least I might have a better chance of controlling it.

Most of the work at this stage is done by a smallish brush, a no. 6, carefully laying in the tones, strengthening here and there and picking out the accents.

The paper is very absorbent and as the colour values dry out, they almost disappear. It is getting a little warmer and visibility more and more murky. I have been here an hour and I cannot do much more that is useful. A horseman on a white horse emerges from behind the pines in the foreground. For a moment the horse stands motionless in the morning sunshine, like a marble equestrian statue, then turns and passes ghostly behind the thin hawthorn bushes. I make a mental note of it; it might be useful. I pack up my gear and walk back to the car.

Plate 80 *Landscape on the Downs* detail.

STUDY: LANDSCAPE

Plate 81 Photograph for *Dog on the Downs*.

Plate 82 *Dog on the Downs I* 1973.
Watercolour 11 × 13⅛ in./279 × 333 mm.
Collection Dr Tench, Florida.

THE PRACTICE OF WATERCOLOUR PAINTING

Plate 83 *Dog on the Downs II* 1973.
Watercolour 11 × 12⅝ in./279 × 321 mm.
Collection Stephen Whitten, Epsom.

Plates 81–84 *Dog on the Downs.*
The drawings of this subject (about six
altogether) were based on photographs
taken on Epsom Downs in the winter of
1973. I had taken a camera on to the Downs
on the morning following a heavy fall of
snow, to gather material for painting. As I
was walking across, an enormous black
Great Dane came towards me. It made
such a marvellous image, this animal
against the snow, that I hastily triggered off
several shots and in my excitement quite
forgot to shut down the aperture to the
correct exposure. In the event it did not
matter much, the bleached-out light areas
lending drama to the situation. All the
watercolours were done later in the studio.
I have painted in the snow, and the colours
froze instead of drying on the paper. When

the painting thawed out later the effects
were extraordinary, not to say catastrophic.
Not to be recommended. All these
watercolours were painted directly on to a
Saunders 90 lb (185 gsm) Not surface paper
with no preliminary drawing. Predictably,
the dog presented the most difficulty.
Holding my breath, I began by painting
the tip of his tail, and working fast and with
a full brush, painted towards his nose. The
problem lay in completing the drawing
before any area had a chance to dry out. In
the third version (Plate 84), the dog, being
slightly smaller, was less of a problem to
paint. By this time he had been joined by a
Dalmatian, whose light coat was invisible
against the snow, I painted only the black
spots, hoping they would by their placing
reveal the form of the dog.

STUDY: LANDSCAPE

Plate 84 *Dog on the Downs III* 1973.
Watercolour $10\frac{7}{8} \times 13\frac{1}{8}$ in./276 $\times$ 333 mm.
Private collection.

SKY STUDIES

Since the majority of students using watercolour are involved in landscape study, the painting of skies is an essential part of the experience and poses particular problems. In every landscape painting there will always be some sky, even if only a very small amount. The sky as the main source of light governs the entire weight of a watercolour painting. So, even though skies can sometimes be very difficult indeed to paint, the painting of them is a useful introduction to the use and control of watercolour and it helps you to understand and cope with problems of space, lighting, tonality, colour and mobility of form. When painting skies, the student encounters most of the technical problems of the medium; because this is a visual experience that requires powers of perception and discernment, it is far more beneficial than those sometimes advocated exercises where you are encouraged to place random marks on paper in a vacuum and are supposed to profit from the experience!

Reproduced in the following pages are a number of sky studies that I have made from time to time. You will see that

Colour Plate 9 *Landscape at Sennen Cove*
1976. Watercolour $10\frac{1}{2} \times 13\frac{1}{2}$ in./266
$\times$ 342 mm. Author's collection.

Colour Plate 10 *Landscape on the Downs*
1976. Watercolour 14 × 17½ in./356
× 444 mm. Author's collection.

Plate 85 *Evening sky study—landscape
under snow.* Watercolour 10⅜ × 21 in./
264 × 533 mm. Author's collection.
Paper, 90lb Not surface. Colours—indigo,
violet, raw sienna, sepia. Paper was damped
in advance. The grey tones were brushed
in at the top, from left to right, and the
dark mass of cloud in the centre was
put in at the same time, its edges melting
into the surrounding area. The colour
changes subtly as one descends the paper,
moving to golden light in the centre on
the horizon. It was allowed to dry, then
after damping the surface lightly, some
darker violet tones at the low right were
brushed in and dark belts of trees were
painted against this. No retouching took
place.

Plate 86 *Epsom Downs—evening sky.*
Watercolour 8 × 22 in./203 × 558 mm.
Author's collection.
This was painted on watercolour board
(paper pasted on card.) There is a golden
light in the sky with mist lying over the
Downs and thick in the valley. The tones
are soft and diaphanous; colours of gold,
pale rose, silver grey and bronze. It was
painted in one go on the spot; because of
the humidity, the drying out was a
problem and I had to keep the water
content down. The trees I brushed in
stiffly while the ground was still wet.

STUDY: LANDSCAPE

Plate 87 H.M.S. Vanguard *being towed away from Portsmouth harbour to the breaker's yard, 1960*. Watercolour 11½ × 15 in./ 292 × 381 mm. Author's collection.
The Admiralty wrote to me in 1960 asking me to do a series of watercolours of the *H.M.S. Vanguard* before she was broken up. The old battleship, little more than a shell now, was towed away by tugs to Scapa Flow for final dismemberment.
As she made her way out past Spithead, a lowering sky moved over from the west as if a gigantic curtain was being drawn across. It was the end of a chapter, she had shown long service and her guns had never been fired in anger.
The Navy put a pinnace at my disposal and a naval photographer and I built up the drawing with the aid of sketches and photographs.

in this diverse collection of skies, the different treatments used have had a varying degree of success. You will notice, for example, how different a sky can become at sunset, in the space of a few minutes.

Some words of advice when painting skies:
(a) Because the main problem is one of control, prepare your paper well in advance, and do not work too large.
(b) Choose a subject to begin with which does not contain too much contrast.
(c) Examine the subject carefully before starting. Try to determine the basic position involved i.e. position of the sun, directional movement of clouds, build-up of tones, and whether these tones go from light to dark, or vice versa.
(d) Do not try to copy every pattern of cloud but extract what you consider to be the essential elements.
(e) Damp the paper in advance if you are working on a passage where you do not want hard edges to the washes of colour.
(f) At the beginning, work from top to bottom, and from light to dark, until you have adequate control of the medium.

Plate 88 *Sky study, after Constable*. Water-colour $9\frac{3}{8} \times 13\frac{1}{2}$ in./239 × 343 mm. Author's collection.

This is a free adaptation after an oil sketch by Constable of a rainstorm falling at sea. Paper, 72lb Not surface. Colours—raw sienna, rose madder, viridian, prussian blue, indigo.

A pale mixed wash, sienna to rose, was laid over the paper and allowed to dry. The paper was then damped slightly and with a large brush the rain clouds hatched in vigorously. The dark sea was laid in with indigo full strength.

Plate 89 *Evening sky studies I and II.*
Watercolour 4⅜ × 10¾ in./111 × 273 mm.
and 4⅛ × 10¾ in./105 × 273 mm.
Author's collection.

These were both painted at the same time.
No. 1 is looking into the sun—a yellow
glow surrounds it—and there is a pale
rose to the right, overhead dark indigo
clouds are moving and a gap in the cloud
to the right shows a sharp edge of cloud.
A purple grey band of cloud lies at the
foot.

The second drawing was made shortly
afterwards. The sun had vanished from
view leaving a yellow to pink glow in the
sky. A deep bank of violet grey cloud was
moving up from the horizon. This was
painted against a slightly damp surface
so that the colour drained away towards
the bottom. I increased the strength of
colour little by little, making it fractionally darker and cooler as I did so. A tinge
of Chinese white in the mixture assisted
the general opacity of the lower, as opposed
to the upper, layers of the drawing.

Plate 90 *Thermal*. Watercolour $7\frac{1}{2} \times 10$ in./ 190 × 253 mm. Author's collection. It was a hot day and a solitary, kidney-shaped cloud floated overhead—it was perhaps more reminiscent of a large jelly-fish with antennae of vapour trailing beneath it. The top edge was sharper against the blue and the lower edges melted away: this posed a nice problem of painting into both dry and damp surfaces. Vapour trails from aircraft criss-crossed the edges and these were lifted out with a sharp knife.

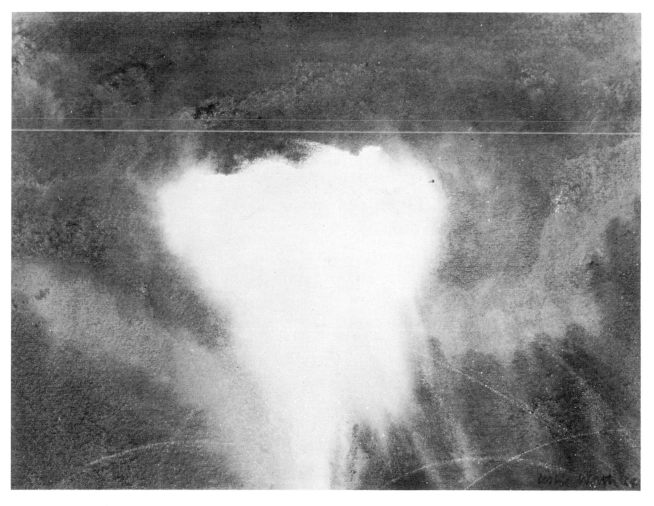

95

Plate 91 *Sky study, looking north over Epsom.* Watercolour $14\frac{7}{8} \times 22\frac{1}{8}$ in./ 378×562 mm. Author's collection. This study was made on the Downs in July 1976. It was a hot, oppressive day with a hint of thunder. The atmosphere was opaque and visibility low; far and middle distances were lost in a leaden haze. A gap appearing in the cloud overhead was actually disappearing and it became more cloudy as I worked. My aim was more to suggest the intervening layers of atmosphere than to explicitly describe cloud forms as such, so the insistence is on overlapping values of colour and I endeavoured to describe space by as close a relationship of tones as I could. The heat dried the colour out fast and I had to repeatedly damp the surface with a sponge; there is a certain murkiness in the result which displeases me, although it is somewhat in character with the day. I worked from the centre of the paper, radiating out towards the edges, and the focal point was suggested by the distant tower block in the centre.

Plate 92 *The Boating Lake*. Watercolour
14⅝ × 21⅜ in./372 × 543 mm. Author's
collection.
Paper, 72lb Not surface. Colours—
Winsor orange, sienna, Chinese vermilion,
madder, prussian blue, violet, sepia.
The paper was damped overall. The
colour of the sky was brushed in from the
top, and descending, I covered the whole
of the paper surface to unify sky and
ground. The evening light was an apricot
colour with a lighter, more orange glow
near the horizon, and the cloud forms
were soft and melting. I allowed the hard
edges to dry where necessary, but generally
I was painting into a damp surface.
The drawing proceeded from light to
darker colours, with care being taken to
keep the tone values consistent.

Plate 93 *Epsom Downs* 1972. Chalk drawing
11 × 14½ in./279 × 368 mm.

Plate 94 *Epsom Downs* 1972. Chalk drawing
11 × 14½ in./279 × 368 mm.

STUDY: LANDSCAPE

5 The subject

What is poetry? To begin with I think we shall clear the ground a little if we cease to regard it as being exclusively the property of literature. True, it may be a property of literature, but it is also found in painting, and, for that matter, leaving all the arts aside, in nature.

Forrest Reid

I don't really believe that there are good subjects, only good paintings, and much energy, boot leather and petrol has been expended looking for 'good subjects', when given insight, a modicum of technical control and sense of order or design, almost any subject is worthy material for painting.

Painting is a vehicle of language and like any sort of communication it has its structure and content and scale, and this may be embodied in an endless variety of forms. It may be formed by study and observation and it requires continuous practice. Earlier I advised students to study all types of art and I still think this is essential for a deeper understanding of the scope of painting: it opens our pores to the influence of art.

What prompts our responses and makes us react to situations or stimuli is embedded deep in our experiences and may not be easily analysed. It is the stuff of our origins and we probably do not recognize it because to us it is the commonplace—'Know thyself' we are advised, and the only way I know of doing this is to look at what is familiar and explore that for subject matter. This will furnish you with material which you can manage because you know it, and in turn it will convince others by its quality of conviction.

I have heard students regret that their work was not 'original' as they describe it. I think they confuse this with novelty or innovation, which is not the same thing. Perhaps they should consider the elements of the word 'originality'—'origin - ality' and begin from there—starting with what they know and understand, because it has been their own experience.

Many artists both past and present have done this and sometimes it has led to neglect by the public simply because the commonplace did not find itself within conventional canons of taste. Consider Constable, for instance, one of the most 'original' of English painters, whose qualities were often unacceptable for that very reason—but whose art very definitely grew from the roots of his own experience.

This familiar extract from one of his letters to Archdeacon Fisher in 1821 illustrates his attitude well and sets the seal on his identity for all time.

> . . . But the sound of water escaping from mill-dams etc.,
> willows, old rotten planks, slimy posts, and brick-work,
> I love such things. . . . As long as I do paint I shall never
> cease to paint such places. . . . Still I should paint my own
> places best; painting is with me but another word for
> feeling and I associate 'my careless boyhood' with all that
> lies on the banks of the Stour; those scenes made me a
> painter and I am grateful. . . .

So I repeat, paint what you know and paint it well!

Of course painting may find its subject matter in other areas than those of visual experience. The late John Minton said that he found the sound of ships' sirens coming from the river particularly evocative, and frequently painters have turned to literature for inspiration—and literature has found inspiration in painting also. An example is a section of a poem based on Pieter Brueghel's painting *The Fall of Icarus:*

> In Breughel's *Icarus*, for instance: how everything turns
> away
> Quite leisurely from the disaster; the ploughman may
> Have heard the splash, the forsaken cry,
> But for him it was not an important failure; the sun shone
> As it had to on the white legs disappearing into the green
> Water; and the expensive delicate ship that must have seen
> Something amazing, a boy falling out of the sky,
> Had somewhere to get to and sailed calmly on.
>   W. H. Auden, 'Musée des Beaux Arts'

Some years ago I did a drawing by the sea in Devonshire, only a a small sketch, and it reminded me afterwards of this poem. Later I used it as a basis for a painting of 'Comus' by John Milton—so oddly enough the wheel had moved full circle; painting—poem—poem—painting.

Poetry and watercolour seem to have a particular affinity. It is something to do with the scale and brevity of both forms. They are both intimate and are not designed for the mass audience, but rather for private contemplation. And also there are links with illustration and the book form which has in the past and today used the medium of watercolour for expression.

Plate 95 *Icarus Landscape* 1968. Pencil drawing 5½ × 7 in./140 × 178 mm.

I have often used poems or prose as a vehicle for painting, not necessarily as an illustration but more in order to establish a parallel mood in another medium. There is an immediacy about watercolour used imaginatively which is capable of evoking both strong and subtle shades of expression with the minimum of fuss or preparation—and permits one to get to the heart of the matter without the necessity of an elaborate procedure.

Watercolour has a special ability to describe a quality of light. Perhaps it derives from its own nature—that of colour washes through which light is reflected. I believe so. But whatever the cause, the fact is undeniable, and because our own psychology readily equates 'mood' with qualities of light, as in:

Gloom/despair/melancholy = dark/low key/opaque
Joy/exultation   = light/high key/luminous

so the subtle use of light nuances from opaque to translucent, dark to light, may express changes of mood. This correspondence of light to mood has been used in literature as in painting.

Perhaps it was this parallel mode of expression that, some years ago, interested me in making some drawings based on Dante's *Inferno*—some of which are reproduced here. (Plates 96–101; Colour Plate 11.)

We were spending a holiday in Boscastle in North Cornwall and, just before we left for Cornwall, I tossed an old copy of a translation of Dante's *Inferno* into the suitcase almost as an afterthought.

We were unlucky, the first week of our fortnight's holiday was wet, as it can only be in the West Country. Unwilling prisoners, we sat indoors and watched the rain sweeping inland

Plate 96 Leslie Worth *Dante meets the Leopard* 1968. Watercolour and pencil 10½ × 13½ in./267 × 343 mm. Private collection.
The time is early in the morning, dawn is breaking, the poet emerges from the dark wood in which he was lost during the night. He meets a leopard at the foot of the hill. (*The Inferno*, Canto I.)

Little preliminary work was done before beginning the drawing. As in all these drawings, the paper was a lightweight cartridge, in a sketchbook. I painted directly into the book, trying to establish the mood of the painting by quality of lighting and weather, and drawing the supporting incidents in afterwards.

in great grey sheets. Looking for some diversion I picked up the *Inferno* and began reading it. It was an edited version of a translation made in the middle of the nineteenth century by Dr John Carlyle, Thomas Carlyle's younger brother, the original was almost seven hundred years old; but it had, for me anyway, lost none of its power. I became more and more absorbed in it, the clarity and force of its vision and its graphic descriptions held my attention.

I read it for some time without seriously thinking of trying to commit my impressions to paper. Indeed when the idea first came, I quickly dismissed it, thinking of the illustrious precedents —Blake, Delacroix, Gustave Doré among them—paralysing competition. However, eventually, more out of curiosity to see if it was possible to realize my impressions on paper, I began to make some drawings.

I had a new sketchbook to hand, measuring about ten inches by fifteen, of rather thin, smooth paper, far from ideal, but readily available. Working lightly with pencil and then using watercolour I began. In order to fix the particular incidents described in the poem I scribbled in the relevant passages in Italian and English and ascribed the Canto number.

THE SUBJECT

Plate 97 *The Trimmers* 1968. Watercolour and pencil 10½ × 14 in./267 × 356 mm. Collection Madame Beek, The Hague.
The scene is set on a vast plain over which a drizzle is falling. A vast throng of spirits, in great confusion and tormented by hornets and wasps, are following a flag. These are the souls of people who in this life followed neither good nor evil and cared only for themselves. Dante describes the miserable procession, '. . . Behind it came so long a train of people that I should never have believed death had undone so many.' (*The Inferno*, Canto III.)

Plate 98 *Charon* 1968. Watercolour and Pencil 11½ × 15¼ in./292 × 387 mm. Collection Theodore Rousseau, Metropolitan Museum, New York.
Dante and Virgil have now come to the banks of the river Acheron, over which the demon Charon ferries the souls of the damned into Hell. A vast crowd of sinners weeping for their fate are assembled on the bank. The bark bearing Charon emerges out of the gloom. He is an old man with white hair and burning eyes, and he cries, 'Woe unto you, depraved spirits, hope not ever to see Heaven, I come to lead you to eternal darkness; into fire and ice.' (*The Inferno, Canto III.*)

The colour is dark and oppressive, chiefly a mixture of sepia and indigo. Two versions of this were done. The first, which was less satisfactory, I destroyed.

Plate 99 *The Carnal Sinners* 1968.
Watercolour and pencil 10½ × 14 in./
267 × 356 mm. Collection Arnold Fawcus,
Paris.
The spirits who in this life were dominated
by lust are blown around by a furious wind,
'like starlings in the cold season, in a large
and crowded troop'. Among them Dante
recognizes Paolo and Francesca—who speaks
the line '. . . there is no greater pain than,
in misery, to recall a happy time.' (*The
Inferno*, Canto V.)
 This drawing proved to be one of the
most difficult, partly on account of the
sobering memory of distinguished
precedents and partly because of the
problem of the delicate balance between the
presence of the figures and the furious
atmosphere, which was difficult to resolve.
I tried several versions and finally (for all
its faults) settled on this. The colour is again
largely monochromatic, of cold greys.

I carried out about a dozen drawings initially, but eventually drew twenty. I will describe something of the considerations that went into their making.

The one element which impressed me above all was that of light. It runs through all the poem like a binding thread. At times ashen, luminous, searing, horrific, it establishes the mood of each situation and symbolizes the plight of the sinners imprisoned therein. The poem starts with the rising sun and ends with starlight. It begins in a dark wood—early in the morning, 'In the middle of the journey of our life, I found myself in a dark wood, where the straight way was lost,' and it ends with the poet emerging from Hell into the clear beauty of an evening, '. . . and thence we issued out, again to see the stars'.

The first drawing (Canto I) depicts Dante emerging from the shadow of the wood and meeting the leopard (a symbol of his native city, Florence), 'And behold, almost at the commencement of the steep, a Leopard, light and very nimble, which was covered with spotted hair'. The morning sunlight is breaking over the mountain, the light is soft and an early lark is ascending.

Plate 100 *The Gluttonous* 1968. Watercolour
and pencil 11½ × 15¼ in./292 × 387 mm.
Collection Bruce Howe, New York.
Dante and Virgil are in the third circle of
Hell, which is the appointed place for those
who have set their hearts upon the lowest
sort of animal gratification. An eternal
storm of heavy hail, foul water and snow
pours down upon the spirits, who are
further tormented by the three-headed
monster Cerberus, who tears them
piecemeal. 'Large hail and turbid water and
snow pour down upon the darksome air;
the ground on which it falls emits a putrid
smell.' (*The Inferno*, Canto IV.)

   This drawing is of a sickly yellowish
colour.

Plate 101 Study for *The Rivers of Hell*
(Colour Plate 11) 1968. Pencil 5½ × 7½ in./
139 × 190 mm.

Colour Plate 11 *Dante's Inferno—The Rivers of Hell* 1970. Watercolour 10½ × 13½ in./266 × 342 mm. Author's collection.

Colour Plate 12 *Volcano, Island of Surtsey*
1973. Watercolour 11 × 14½ in./279
× 368 mm. Author's collection.

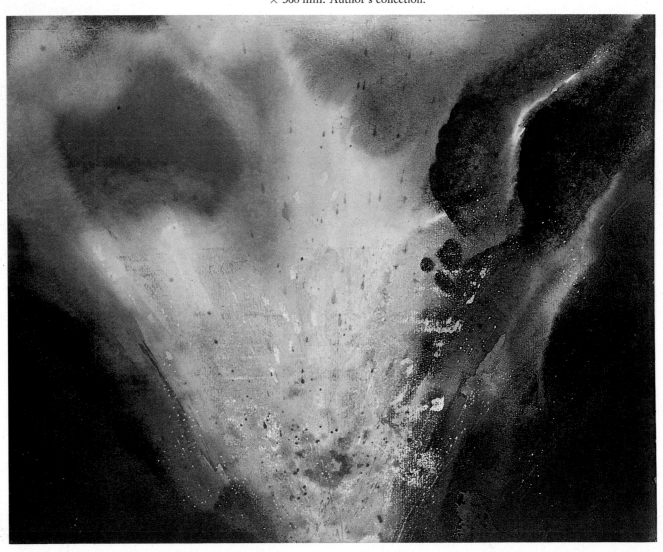

Moonshot watercolour sketches

At Christmas 1968 the Apollo 8 moonshot with the three astronauts, Borman, Lovell and Anders aboard the capsule, circled the moon and successfully returned to Earth, where they were picked up in the Pacific by the U.S. Carrier *Yorktown*. Like a lot of other people, I stayed up late to watch this on the television, and while watching this in the early stages of the production, I realised that the Pacific dawn, when the splash down was to be made, would make some excellent pictures. I made rapid pencil notes on a pad, there and then, in front of the television, and the whole story of the splash down, the pick-up by helicopter and the landing on the deck of the aircraft carrier unfolded. In some instances I had to work very fast because the television picture changed very quickly. This demanded a lot of concentration as the detail and structure of each composition had to be put down on paper very speedily indeed.

Plate 102 *Waiting—Dawn 27/12/1968.* Pen and watercolour 3½ × 5 in./ 89 × 122 mm.
Pen is used on the caps of the sailors in the foreground—sparingly as in all the drawings, so that the medium does not intrude. For the rest, watercolour was used directly on a medium weight paper.

Plate 103 *Dawn—U.S. Carrier* Yorktown *—ship's company waiting.* Pen and watercolour 3½ × 5 in./89 × 122 mm.
A cold light over the sea, dark but getting lighter. A handful of officers peer into the distance to catch a glimpse of the helicopters which have picked up the astronauts.

THE SUBJECT

Plate 104 *Waiting for astronauts—6.15 am.*
Pen and watercolour $3\frac{1}{2} \times 5$ in./
89×122 mm.

Plate 105 *Flight-deck, U.S. Carrier*
Yorktown *27/12/1968.* Pen and watercolour
$3\frac{1}{2} \times 5$ in./89×122 mm.
A group of seamen stand in the shadow
of the superstructure from which large
search-lights blaze.

Plate 106 *Three helicopters on the horizon.* Pen
and watercolour $3\frac{1}{2} \times 5$ in./ 89×122 mm.
A tense moment. Three tiny specks just
above the horizon indicate the returning
helicopters.

Plate 107 *The first helicopter circles the* Yorktown. Pen and watercolour 3½ × 5 in./89 × 122 mm.

Plate 108 *Helicopter '66' comes to rest.* Pen and watercolour 3½ × 5 in./ 89 × 122 mm.

Plate 109 *The astronauts pass into the elevator.* Pen and watercolour 3½ × 5 in./ 89 × 122 mm.
The last glimpse that the television cameras had of the astronauts before they disappeared into the interior of the ship.

THE SUBJECT

I was so pleased with the set of watercolour drawings of the Apollo 8 splash down that I set out to do the same task again in July 1969 when the first successful landing was made on the moon. Like many other people in Britain, I had to stay up for most of the night in order to catch this historic moment on television. In the series of paintings here, the light, as you can see, is very harsh indeed. The whole series of paintings was executed in monochrome using Payne's grey as a base. Because the television cameras were fixed, I had longer to work at each drawing than on the Apollo 8 series. All the work I did in front

Plate 110 *Destination moon*. Watercolour
$3\frac{5}{8} \times 4\frac{3}{8}$ in./92 × 112 mm.
The moon as seen from the approaching space capsule.

Plate 111 *Lunar surface*. Watercolour
$4 \times 4\frac{1}{2}$ in./102 × 114 mm.
The module is just coming in to land and this shot was transmitted back as the camera scanned the surface.

of the television was in the form of pencil sketches which were later turned into watercolour drawings. This set of drawings demanded both accuracy and economy of brush stroke, because I was working in monochrome and the light on the moonscape was so harsh that the tonal qualities needed very careful handling. It is interesting to note that in all these the sky, of course, was very dark, almost black, and yet within this blackness there was room for sensitivity of tone.

Plate 112 *Armstrong descends.* Watercolour 4 × 4½ in./102 × 114 mm.
Against the brightly lit curving horizon of the moon, 'Buzz' Aldrin's leg is silhouetted. It occasioned the now famous remark 'one small step for a man, one large step for Mankind'.

Plate 113 *Walking on the moon.*
Watercolour 4 × 4½ in./102 × 114 mm.
The first tentative steps taken on the moon's surface—not so much steps as bounces, as the two astronauts, like rubber dolls, bounded around in a circle in the weightless atmosphere.

THE SUBJECT

Plate 114 *Solar experiment*. Watercolour
4 × 4½ in./102 × 114 mm.
The simple experimental apparatus is here
being set up. The astronaut in the
foreground with his back to the camera,
is, if I remember correctly, busy photo-
graphing his companion. The time was
precisely 5.06 am. 21st July 1969.

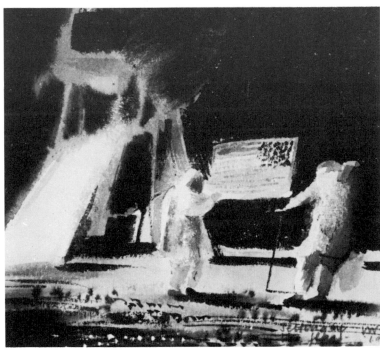

Plate 115 *Setting up the flag*. Watercolour
4 × 4½ in./102 × 114 mm.
In the reduced gravity atmosphere of the
moon, the American flag sticks out like
a cardboard sheet.

Plate 116 *Armstrong photographs Aldrin.*
Watercolour 4 × 4½ in./102 × 114 mm.
Armstrong on the left is preparing to
photograph Aldrin who, turning round,
comes bounding towards him.

6 Body colour

Gouache, gwash, *n*. a method of watercolour painting with opaque colours, mixed with water, honey and gum, presenting a dead surface: work painted according to this method. (Fr.)

Chambers's Twentieth Century Dictionary

Gouache has a brilliant light-reflecting quality of a different and distinctive nature; it lies in the paint surface itself; its whiteness or brightness comes from the use of white pigments. It is most popularly used in a high chromatic key or in strong contrasts of values. The medium is highly appropriate for use in creating the effect of spontaneity and an *alla prima* effect. The average gouache painting is done on less roughly textured paper than the average watercolour, and painters often use tinted paper, or start with a partial foundation painting of watercolour as is sometimes done with pastel.

Ralph Mayer,
The Artist's Handbook of Materials and Techniques

This book has been largely concerned with the methods and techniques of 'pure' watercolour, unalloyed with the addition of body colour, which has long been an anathema to many purists. However, I hold no particular scruples about it myself and it would be improper to end without some mention of the use of body colour, 'gouache' as it is called.

In gouache the basic colour pigment is ground with a mixture of precipitated chalk and bound with a solution of gum. The proportions of pigment, chalk and gum vary from colour to colour.

Watercolour with the addition of body colour is historically the older method. The Egyptians used a form of opaque watercolour, tempera or distemper (see Introduction), and it has been used in a variety of ways throughout history. The Elizabethan

Colour Plate 13 Jane Taylor *A Room in Montparnasse* 1952. Watercolour 14¼ × 18¼ in./368 × 463 mm. Artist's collection.

This was painted away from the spot in the studio, from a smaller painting which was actually carried out in the room in Montparnasse. It is broadly painted, conceived as a sketch, in contrast to the more complete original.

It is painted on a grey sugar paper which may be seen through some of the more loosely painted areas. The colours used were watercolours to which Chinese white was added.

The main features of the design were first drawn in with pink using a small brush, then the main colour areas were brushed in broadly to establish the composition. The green areas of the balconied windows, the wall and carpet were then painted in, the carpet being worked over several times to achieve a rich, dark surface. The check pattern of the cloth, as the centre of the design, was more elaborately built up with crossing lines and the interstices picked out in lighter tones. Finally the bottles and lemons were added and the curved lines of the iron balconies drawn in.

The artist sometimes uses a light wax polish on the final painting to give a richer surface. That was not done in this painting and care should be exercised when it is done or the darker tones may appear 'jumpy'.

Colour Plate 14 *Early Morning at Vellen-dreath* 1975. Watercolour 16 × 21 in./ 406 × 533 mm. Author's collection.

Colour Plate 15 *Genesis—the Creation of Living Creatures* 1974. Watercolour 10 × 13½ in./254 × 342 mm. Author's collection.

Colour Plate 16 *The Angel standing in the Sun* 1975. Watercolour 10 × 14 in./266 × 356 mm. Author's collection.

miniature painters Nicholas Hilliard and Isaac Oliver used it, as did the Indian and Persian painters.

The nineteenth-century artist Samuel Palmer used the rich texture of the medium to an unrivalled degree in his Shoreham paintings, and in this century artists such as Frances Hodgkins, Keith Vaughan and Graham Sutherland have been identified with it. My wife, Jane Taylor, has used it almost exclusively. One of her paintings, *A Room in Montparnasse*, is reproduced in Colour Plate 13.

The medium on the whole has been more exploited on the Continent than in Britain or America, and there are several brands of gouache colours readily available in France, Holland and Germany and, I believe, in Italy (called *guazzo*). There is a very comprehensive British range called 'Designers' Colours' manufactured by Winsor & Newton. They possess a clarity and strength (with the exception of the greens, which are lacking in body) which most students would find very satisfactory.

Body colour is a very broad term. Turner used it a great deal, in a range from the addition of body colour to an otherwise transparent watercolour (some of his Rhineland drawings and drawings at Farnley Hall exemplify this) to later drawings, where he used body colour on a grey-blue or brown paper.

Many artists prefer to use watercolours with the addition of Chinese white, this allows a greater range of transparency to opacity and produces softer, less chalky qualities.

As noted in the quotation from Ralph Mayer at the head of this chapter, a tinted paper, such as one of the range offered by the Ingres papers is good to work with. Failing this a broad build-up of the main features of the design in transparent water colour is a great help, and interesting results may be produced by under-painting some areas with a contrasting or complementary colour, then hatching or scumbling over the top with more opaque passages, allowing some of the under colour to come through and play its part. Much of the skill in handling gouache lies in the balance achieved between thick and thin areas. Too thick an application is difficult to handle, looks leaden in appearance and is inclined to flake off; too thin an application gives a muddy, granular look to the colour.

Students would be advised to experiment with the medium until they discover the right 'feel' for it. Using card to paint on is very helpful. Off-cuts from tinted mounting card are very good to use. If one uses strawboard, the warm colour is a nice counterbalance to the characteristic 'greys' of the gouache colour. Should this appear too absorbent in surface, a thin size solution (twelve parts to one part glue or gelatine size) brushed on and allowed to dry will remedy this.

Students who may be interested in preparing their own colours are advised to consult a good standard reference book. (See bibliography.)

BODY COLOUR

Plate 117 Samuel Palmer *The Bright Cloud*
1829. Chinese white, pen and sepia wash
9 × 12 in./229 × 305 mm. Tate Gallery,
London.

This was painted when Palmer was living
at Shoreham in Kent. Spiritually under the
influence of William Blake and imbued
with the pastoral visions of Virgil and
Milton, in the few years in which he lived
at Shoreham he created a series of drawings
which for passionate intensity and power of
design have few parallels in English painting.
The fervour could not last for ever and it
burnt itself out. His later work was overlaid
with detail and he lost sight of the
rapturous simplicity exemplified in this
watercolour. The design is built up in three
sections held together with analogous
curves: 1. The field and sheep in the
foreground. 2. The trees in the middle
distance. 3. The cumulus clouds.

7 Presentation

So far in this book we have considered the many aspects of producing watercolours, the basic materials and studies and the production of completed works of various sorts.

The advice given so far would be incomplete without considering the presentation and care of the finished work. Exhibiting needs careful preparation. Even if your plans are more modest, keeping the work in respectable insularity is preferable to cutting it roughly off the drawing board and pushing it away in a portfolio or drawer. Whatever you do, let us consider first of all the care of the finished drawings.

Remove them carefully from the drawing board. Sometimes, if you painted on lightweight paper, the gum from the gummed-paper strip holding the paper to the board may seep under the drawing, gumming it irregularly but, unfortunately, effectively, to the board. This has happened to me more than once when I have been using a thin Ingres paper. If this occurs, take a thin-bladed, flexible knife and, pressing it flat, gently ease the paper from the board.

One other source of danger to be prepared against is leaving old pieces of gumstrip clinging to the board. These can sometimes attach themselves to the reverse side of the drawing, doing considerable damage when you lift the drawing off. Keep the board clean!

When I cut the drawing off the board I try as far as possible to cut opposite sides before releasing the paper. Sometimes the paper will contract slightly when the tension is released, and releasing opposite sides reduces the likelihood of its tearing suddenly. Having removed the drawing from the board, trim up the edges with a sharp knife, straight-edge and set-square so that the corners are true right angles. This is most important. You will be gratified to observe the improvement in your drawing now it is separated from the surround of a discoloured drawing board. It will look better if you now drop it down on to a clean white sheet of paper.

If you plan to do no more with your drawings than this, then at least inter them in your drawer or folio, decently. Keep them flat, preferably with thin paper between them (tissue paper is the best) and keep them free from damp or dirt. If on the other hand you have aspirations to exhibiting your work, then you must consider the question of mounting and framing.

The simplest and no doubt most satisfactory solution to this problem as regards final results is to take your drawings along to a reputable framer, and choose a suitable frame and mount your work and get him to do it for you. However, this always costs money and can be quite expensive. So, if you think you possess the necessary skill, you may choose to do your own mounting and framing. There are books on the market setting out in detail the intricacies of the framer's craft, and in this brief chapter I cannot hope to rival those, but I will outline the basic procedure for the benefit of students who may be interested.

MOUNTING AND FRAMING

Materials

1. Card—for backing (laying) the drawing and for the mount. (Mat in the US.)
2. Picture glass. This is lightweight glass. Some people like a non-reflective glass (polarized) to prevent glare. I do not like it myself. I think it gives the work an unfortunate 'plastic' appearance but this is a matter of personal taste. Clear perspex may be used for some works. It does not break but can scratch and discolour and is more expensive than glass.
3. Backing board. Usually hardboard, or Masonite, a resin-bonded composition board, approximately $\frac{1}{8}$ in. (3 or 5 mm) thick. Sometimes a thin fibre board may be used but this offers less protection.
4. The frame. Suitable moulding may be purchased in lengths from a stockist or wholesale importer. It is also possible to use lightweight aluminium angle of various weights and sizes if it is suitable for the work.
5. Sundry materials include:
    Paste, gumstrip or masking tape.
    Panel pins or moulding pins for fixing the backing board.
    Framers often use flat, triangular-shaped, metal 'sprigs' which are discharged with a special gun into the edge of the frame at the back, pinning the board into position.
    Rings for attaching to the back of the frame.
    Nylon cord, wall-hooks.

An effective method of framing a simple modern watercolour, is to lay the work on plain card, on a $\frac{1}{2}$ in. (12 mm) sheet of ply or blockboard, cover with a sheet of perspex and secure at the edges with mirror clips. (The most common are nylon clips resembling in shape the letter 'E' with the central bar removed, and there are also 'L'-shaped clips which can be screwed to the edge of the board.) Care must be taken to ensure that the combined thickness of board, card and perspex fits tightly into the opening of the clips.

Mounting card is built up in thicknesses and it can be bought in thicknesses of 4 sheet, 6 sheet, 8 sheet, etc. according to one's requirements. Cheaper card is manufactured from wood-pulp and will discolour, becoming 'brownish' in time. The best, and obviously more expensive card is made from rag boards. Framers use these and they do not discolour. Mounting card usually has a paper surface 'laid' on. This varies in colour and texture from white through ivory and a large, often attractive, range of colours to black. A good framer carries a 'swatch' of these cards and will show you samples. You may even obtain a sample stock of cards from a manufacturer.

Some very attractive mounting cards have linen or canvas pasted on to the surface. This can be very effective when judiciously used. The type of linen-cloth used by bookbinders can be useful for this.

Tools

1. Mount-cutting knife. There are a number of proprietary knives on the market. It is possible to make one by inserting a mount-cutter's blade into a wooden handle or you can buy a knife with detachable blades. Spare blades are obtainable from hardware stores. The main disadvantage is that the blades are inclined to be too flexible for precision work and a stiffer blade is preferable.
2. Steel straight-edge. A good heavy one is necessary and it should not be too thin or the knife may jump over the edge under pressure.
3. Large set-square.

Plate 118 This photograph shows the Ulmia mitre saw in position on the bench. Five positions are possible, and here it is held in a predetermined position for cutting at 45°. Note the mitre cramp in the background with a section of the moulding in position.

PRESENTATION

4. Ruling pen. For wash-lines if you are interested in using these.
5. Adhesive. PVA glue in a plastic dispenser is useful. Many framers use this in place of the traditional starch-based paste.
6. Masking tape, gumstrip or other adhesive tape.
7. Glass cutter. This is useful if you consider yourself competent to use one. It is not easy, although it looks deceptively so in the hands of the practised glazier. You may be well advised to leave it to the expert.
8. Tack hammer and panel pins.
9. Mitre saw. A simple mitre block may be used successfully if care is exercised. There are a number of proprietary cutters on the market. If you plan to go into the business seriously it would be wise to invest in an Ulmia mitreing saw. Made in Germany (ULM), this is marketed in Britain by Tyzacks of London. Essentially it is a saw operated on a sort of trombone slide and may be set in a number of positions. (See Plate 118.)
10. Mitre shaver. This is an optional extra for the devotee—a fixed bench top guillotine which shaves wooden sections to a predetermined angle. Rather expensive. (See Plate 119.)

Plate 119 The mitre shaver in action. There are two vertical blades which slide on a bed when the lever is pulled. Notice the two curved vertical metal stops against which the wood is held. The angle may be changed by releasing the locks and adjusting the stops on the curved slots.

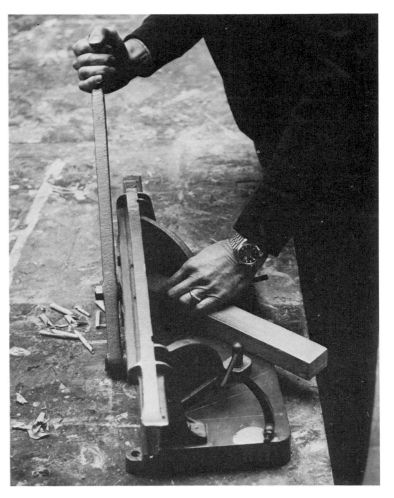

11. Sundries include tenon saw, chisels, glue, panel pins, etc. Most important of course is a place where you can do all this, with a work-bench of a convenient height and size. Good light is essential and you may find an adjustable lamp a useful investment if you envisage having to work by artificial light.

Procedure

1. Trim the drawing to size, ensuring with the aid of a square that the corners are true right angles.

2. Take a sheet of stiff white card. If you use an off-white or tinted card you may find it a good idea to leave approximately $\frac{1}{4}$ in. (6 mm) of white surrounding the drawing instead of bringing the edge of the mount right up to the drawing—this usually imparts a little extra vitality to the drawing and sets it back somewhat. Turn the drawing face downwards and with the plastic dispenser (if you are using a proprietary PVA glue) spread a thin bead of glue all round the back of the drawing about $\frac{1}{8}$ in. (3 mm) from the edge. Moisten your finger tip and spread the line of glue around, this ensures an even coverage and prevents a small ridge appearing on the front when the glue sets.

3. Turn the drawing face upwards in the centre of the card and with a piece of clean paper over it to protect the surface, brush gently outwards from the centre with your hand. This prevents any air-bubbles forming under the drawing. Make certain that the edges of the drawing are glued down firmly all round.

    If the drawing has cockled a bit before laying it, it may help to damp the reverse side a little (don't overdo it) with a sponge. This will cause the paper to expand slightly, and contracting as it will when it dries, it will pull out flat. Leave it under a weight to dry out or it will buckle.

4. The width of the mount depends on the size of the drawing and your personal taste in this matter. I think it better to have too much than too little, but as a general guide, a 3 in. (76 mm) width with $3\frac{1}{2}$ in. (89 mm) at the base is a good universal size. Don't forget to add $\frac{1}{4}$ in. (6 mm) to the window opening all round to allow for a narrow margin of white card to show around the drawing.

5. Lay a piece of card on the bench to cut on. Draw the window opening on the mounting card, making sure that you have sufficient surround for the width of mount. With practice you will just mark neatly with a small + at each corner.

6. Lay the straight-edge against the line and with the knife inclined outward to the right at an angle of approximately 30°, cut into the corner with the point and pull it towards you. Keep the angle constant and be careful not to overshoot the near corner. Repeat on all four sides. You will probably discover that even if you have penetrated the card completely, the corners are still not free. Lift up the card and, keeping the

Plate 120 Angle of knife for cutting mount.

Plate 121 Workshop showing hinged mount and mounting tools on the bench.

same angle, insert the knife and slide it gently towards the corner. This should free the card. If there are any rough edges trim these up. As a general tip, if you have to cut a bevel edge twice then raise the knife to a slightly steeper angle at the second attempt. This will prevent the edge being stepped. If you are nervous about cutting a bevel mount, cut a mount with straight sides by holding the knife vertically. It takes a lot of practice to cut a clean bevel mount accurately. The knife must be absolutely razor sharp and the angle constant.

7. The mount may be secured by running a small amount of glue under it, thereby fixing it to the backing card, or if the backing card is smaller than the outside dimensions of the mount, a length of adhesive tape around the edges will suffice. Make certain that the mount is accurately placed around the drawing

before fixing. A good way of preventing the steel straight-edge from slipping under pressure when you cut the mount is to fix a screw to the far edge of the bench and slot the hole in the straight-edge over this.

Wash-lines

Although not used much in many contemporary paintings, they are appropriate for certain drawings, architectural subjects and so forth. They need to be very well done if they are to be used at all, inferior examples cheapen a drawing.

The student would be advised to examine some good examples and try several experiments before embarking on this enterprise.

The purposes of wash-lines are:

(a) To give 'support' to the drawing by emphasizing the vertical and horizontal aspects.
(b) To slow down the transition from the drawn area to the mount.
(c) To 'pick up' some of the colour characteristics of the drawing and echo them in the border.

Materials. Ruling pen, inks or colour washes in saucers or similar receptacles, brushes, pencil, ruler with bevelled edge.

Points to watch:
(a) The proportion of the intervals between the lines.
(b) The tonality and colours chosen—care being taken that they are appropriate to the drawing.
(c) That you have sufficient colour mixed up to go all round the drawing without having to mix a fresh amount.

Procedure. Assuming that you are all set to start, your materials are ready, your brushes are in good condition (a fine point is essential), enough colour prepared, begin by trying out some

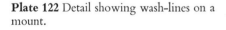

Plate 122 Detail showing wash-lines on a mount.

PRESENTATION

examples of colour on spare pieces of paper, preferably the same colour as the mount.

Gently with a pencil draw the lines around the mount opening, in the proportions you consider satisfactory. Ensure that the corners coincide accurately across the diagonals and that they really are parallel. (Practised framers often make a prick at the corner with a sharp point to mark the position before using the ruling-pen.) Charge the ruling pen with colour or ink and having tried it out on a piece of paper, run it along against the bevelled edge of a rule (with the bevel underneath—or the ink may run back).

Beginning at one corner, working rapidly, lay in your colour band right round to where you started. If you think the initial colour will dry out before you complete the circuit, brush a little clear water into the area before you start in order to avoid a hard edge.

The next task is to cut the moulding.

If you possess or have access to a mitre saw (Plate 118), this part of the operation should not present too much difficulty. It may be worthwhile to experiment on an odd piece of wood to satisfy yourself that the corners are cutting accurately before you embark on the final job. If you use a simple mitre block, then you must be more careful. Sometimes they are not absolutely accurate and you may have to make adjustments.

Plate 123 Selection of frames: *top left* gessoed frame, canvas covered mount; *top right* gilt frame, wash-line mount and black ebony frame (miniature); *bottom left* aluminium frame; *bottom right* wash-lines, gold leaf gessoed on simple wood section frame.

Allow for the thickness of the saw cut and hold or cramp the wood quite still in the block. When all four corners are cut satisfactorily you must pin and glue them. If you can use a special mitre cramp (Plate 118) this is the obvious solution. Cramp two adjacent sections into the mitre cramp until they form a perfect corner under pressure. Release one side and spread on it a thin solution of woodworking glue—replace in the cramp and tighten it. Then, using some 1 in. (25 mm) thin panel pins, pin

selves in such imposed isolation. I am inclined to think that galleries are a necessary evil and that basically painting speaks as individual to individual. I don't deny the usefulness or profitability of the gallery system, I just think that the language of the chamber is not the language of the market place. However, we must learn to walk in the world and to hold our souls inviolate—so take pride in your work and in its presentation, learn what you can from others, strengthen your ideas by evaluating your own contribution against that of your contemporaries, study hard, hold fast to your instincts and good luck to you.

Where you choose to exhibit will depend on your experience and standard, among other things, and there is a wide spectrum of facilities available, from joining the local art society to submitting work to the competition of large open exhibitions and

Plate 126 Drawing for *Semmer Water* 1971. Pencil 4 × 5¼ in./102 × 133 mm.

Plate 127 Drawing for *Semmer Water* 1971. Pencil 4 × 5¼ in./102 × 133 mm.

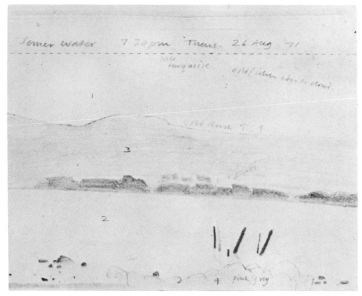

Plate 128 *Semmer Water—Homage to Hokusai*
1972. Watercolour $10\frac{1}{2} \times 13\frac{3}{4}$ in./267 ×
349 mm. Author's collection.
We came across Semmer Water some years
ago when we were staying in Wensleydale
in Yorkshire. A still, saucer-like lake
surrounded by low fells, it was fringed by
delicate reeds and had a mysterious beauty
about it. One could readily understand the
legend that a submerged village lay in its
unruffled depths. The scene had a still,
almost Japanese quality, reminiscent of
landscape prints by Hiroshige and Hokusai.

I did several drawings in a sketchbook
and from these painted a number of
watercolours, of which this is one. The
numerals 1, 2 and 3 in the drawing
illustrated in Plate 127 indicate the main
tonal areas from light to dark. Some notes
of colour are written in for guidance. The
painting followed this drawing fairly
closely, differing only in that I changed the
proportion of the distant fell to the lake to
suggest greater space. A strong blue in the
sky gives way to a pinkish flush. The distant
fell is a restrained madder colour. A
deliberate attempt is made to reduce
incidents to a minimum.

exhibiting societies. Further on is the goal beckoning the aspirant
—the showing of work in celebrated galleries and the final
accolade of the one-man show! A list of exhibiting societies and
general exhibition information can be found on page 135.

Conclusion

I cannot better take my leave of you than in the words
of my friend Archdeacon Fisher . . . 'In my present
perplexity, the recollection comes to my relief that when
any man has given an undivided attention to any one
subject, his audience willingly yield him for his hour the
chair of instruction; he discharges his mind of its
conceptions, and descends from his temporary elevation
to be instructed in his turn by other men.'
> John Constable, at the conclusion of his Fourth and
> Last Lecture at the Royal Institution, 16 June 1836.

In writing this book two main difficulties have presented themselves to me. The first to a large extent exists for all who endeavour to offer advice in the pursuit of art, namely, in the absence of
any central tradition and in the proliferation of so many styles and
approaches, what advice can one give that is relevant? The second
is, what practical advice can one offer concerning the use of a
medium which is basically so simple that it relies for its success
on one's own sensibilities and technical control, possessing as it
does no elaborate or systematic process by which one may govern
its use and behaviour?

Well—'what I have written, I have written', and such advice
as exists, as far as I can offer it, is between the pages of this book.
In answer to the first question, I have endeavoured to set the
practice of watercolour painting in perspective so that by reference
to outstanding examples of the past, involving a variety of techniques, some overriding values may be apparent.

There is no easy pathway to success with the medium. It
requires careful thought, hard work and a basic understanding
of the limitations of the materials. But all this is very enjoyable.
All I can offer you is a lot of concentrated study and a richly
rewarding experience—what more do you want? Above all you
must have a love of watercolour for its own sake. If you have

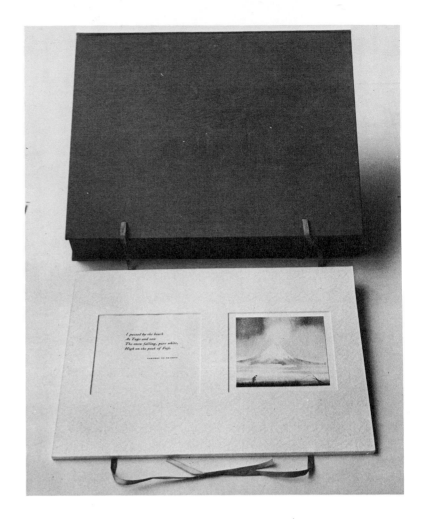

Plate 129 *A Box of Poems* 1974. Mixed media 16 × 12 × 4 in./406 × 305 × 102 mm. Collection J. R. Robertson, Surrey.
For some time I had been interested in the idea of an alternative to the framed watercolour hanging on the wall, and on coming across a modern translation of some early Japanese *haiku* poems I conceived the notion of a sort of package deal. The watercolours were not considered as illustrations to the poems but rather as offering a parallel experience in visual terms, the poem and the painting to be enjoyed together, the one acting as complementary to the other. The box was made by a bookbinder, the text set in Fournier typeface by a typographer.

this you will succeed; if you have not, something essential will always be missing.

I have demonstrated the basic essentials of drawing practice, which is the structure underlying watercolour painting, and a keen sense of observation which informs what we do. I have pointed out the importance of having reliable materials and of organizing them and our work space so that we may obtain the best results. Over all this is our own vision and perception which directs all this to the final end, a language of expression. Here you are on your own and neither I nor anyone else can tell you what you must do.

I have also drawn attention to the importance of design, which is nothing to do with mannerism or affectation, but by which I mean the essential structure of the watercolour drawing, its balance, harmony, relationship of the parts to the whole. I hope the analysis of good drawings here and elsewhere will increase our understanding of the organization of our own drawings.

What has been written is a testimony of one painter writing from the basis of his own experience. It will not necessarily accord with other writers, nor is it by any means the whole story. Finally each one of us must make our own mistakes and

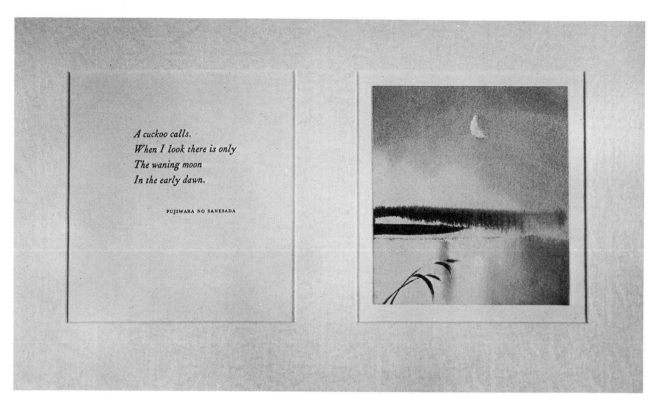

A cuckoo calls.
When I look there is only
The waning moon
In the early dawn.

FUJIWARA NO SANESADA

Plate 130 Detail of *Box of Poems*.

forge our own practice. If what has been said so far helps students already struggling to succeed, and perhaps encourages others who have not used it to explore the possibilities of this delightful medium, I shall be content.

Bibliography

METHODS AND MATERIALS

BAZZI, Maria, *The Artist's Methods and Materials*. John Murray, London, 1960.

DOERNER, Max, *The Materials of the Artist*. Hart-Davies, London, and Harcourt Brace, New York, 1969.

HILER, Hilaire, *Notes on the Technique of Painting*. Faber & Faber, London, 1969.

HILER, Hilaire, *The Painter's Pocket Book of Methods and Materials*. Faber & Faber, London, 1970.

MAYER, Ralph, *The Artist's Handbook of Materials and Techniques*. Faber & Faber, London, 1972 and Viking Press, New York, 1970.

Notes on the Composition and Permanence of Artists' Watercolours. Winsor & Newton, Harrow, Middlesex.

COLOUR SYSTEMS AND ANALYSIS

BIRREN, Faber, *Principles of Colour*. Van Nostrand Reinhold, New York, 1970.

CHEVREUL, M. E., *The Principle of Harmony and Contrast of Colour*. Longman, Brown, Green & Longmans, 1854, and Van Nostrand Reinhold, New York, 1967.

EASTLAKE, Sir Charles, *Goethe's Theory of Colour*. Frank Cass, London, 1967.

ITTEN, Johannes, *The Art of Colour*. Van Nostrand Reinhold, New York, 1961.

MARX, Ellen, *The Contrast of Colours*. Van Nostrand Reinhold, New York, 1973.

MUNSELL, Albert H., *A Grammar of Colour*. Van Nostrand Reinhold, New York, 1970.

OSTWALD, Wilhelm, *The Color Primer*. Van Nostrand Reinhold, New York, 1970.

PAPER

HIGHAM, Robert R. A., *A Handbook of Papermaking*. Oxford University Press, 1963.

STEWART, Derek, *Paper*. A. Wheaton, Exeter, Modern Industries Series, 1969.

GENERAL

BINYON, Laurence, *English Watercolour*, A. & C. Black, London, 1933.

BINYON, Laurence, *Flight of the Dragon*. John Murray, London, 1911.

HARDIE, Martin, *Watercolour Painting in Britain* (3 vols.). B. T. Batsford, London, 1966.

LESLIE, C. R., *Memoirs of the Life of Constable*. Longman, Brown, Green & Longmans, London, 1845, and Phaidon, London, 1951.

List of Suppliers

Painting materials and equipment
Winsor and Newton Ltd, Wealdstone, Harrow, Middlesex.

George Rowney and Co., Bracknell, Berkshire.

C. Roberson and Co., Parkway, London, N.W.1.

Knives, inks, Japanese papers, tools, etc.
T. N. Lawrence and Son, Bleeding Heart Yard, Greville Street, London, W.C.1.

Tools, machines
S. Tyzack and Son, 341 Old Street, London, E.C.1.

Paper suppliers and manufacturers
RWS paper, Crisbrooke, De Wint, etc., J. Barcham Green, Hayle Mill, Maidstone, Kent.

Saunders papers
Inveresk Paper Co., Clan House, Tudor Street, London, E.C.4.

Arches papers (France)
Ploton Sundries, 273 Archway Road, London, N.6.

G. M. Fabriano papers (Italy)
Interprovincial Sales Ltd., Edgware, Middlesex.

Branches of principal artists' colourmen and retailers carry supplies of papers.

Exhibiting

Exhibiting and exhibition information:
Information may be obtained from:

Regional Arts Associations
Federation of British Artists, The Mall, London
Local art galleries and art societies

Magazines:

Arts News and Review
Arts News and Review Year Book
Artist magazine
Leisure Painter and Craftsman
Art and Artists
Studio International

Exhibiting Societies:

Royal Academy of Arts—sending days end of March
Royal Water Colour Society—members only
Royal Scottish Society of Painters in Watercolours—January
Royal Institute of Painters in Watercolours—February
Royal Society of British Artists—May
New English Art Club—October
Royal West of England Academy—October
Royal Cambrian Academy—May

Index